CIVIL WAR MEMOIRS of TWO REBEL SISTERS

WHEN MOLLIE HANSFORD MARRIED DR. JOHN WALLS, SHE moved to the Shenandoah Valley of Virginia, seven miles south of Winchester. There the Civil War raged all around her for four long years.

Her half-sister, Victoria Hansford, in the Kanawha Valley was equally surrounded by the perils of war at Coalsmouth, now St. Albans, West Virginia.

They each recorded their wartime experiences as they could have only been seen through the eyes of a woman.

LIBRARY OF CONGRESS
CATALOG CARD NO. 89-62739

ISBN 0-929521-24-2

PRINTED IN U.S.A.

First Printing   October 1989
Second Printing   May 1990
Third Printing   July 1992

Typography: Arrow Graphics
Layout: Stan Cohen

Published for William D. Wintz
St. Albans, West Virginia

PICTORIAL HISTORIES PUBLISHING CO.
4103 Virginia Ave. SE
Charleston, West Virginia 25304

CONTENTS

FOREWORD

DURING THE CIVIL WAR, MOLLIE HANSFORD WALLS WAS A doctor's wife living at Newtown (now Stephen City), in the Shenandoah Valley of Virginia. She had come there as a bride in 1853 from her old home in Coalsmouth (now St. Albans, West Virginia), located in the Kanawha Valley. Her father, two half brothers, and two half sisters still lived there. Mollie and her sister, Victoria Hansford, each wrote vivid accounts of their stirring wartime experiences.

Victoria was 23, unmarried, and was keeping house for her father when the war began. She and many of her young friends were soon caught up in the excitement and issues of the times, and they quickly became deeply involved in the Confederate cause.

Victoria in the Kanawha Valley and Mollie in the Shenandoah Valley both lived in military hotspots of the war. Although they were located miles apart and were unable to correspond, they often mentioned the same people and events in their writings. For instance, Victoria recorded that in 1861 Captain George Patton, a Charleston lawyer, came to Coalsmouth to raise volunteers for his newly formed company, The Kanawha Riflemen. She described the patriotic scene when the townspeople turned out to hear Patton make a rousing speech and to see her brother, along with other sons of Coalsmouth, sworn into the Confederate Army. She also told how everyone cheered and wept as the boys rode off in a wagon with Captain Patton. The Kanawha Riflemen eventually became Company H of the 22nd Virginia Infantry with Colonel Patton commanding.

Mollie later wrote about the 22nd fighting in the Shenandoah Valley in her neighborhood, and how she managed to see a number of the boys from home. Eight principal battles were fought within a dozen miles of Mollie's house, including those in which the 22nd took part.

It was during the third battle of Winchester that Colonel Patton was fatally wounded while trying to rally his troops against a superior force. He was buried only seven miles from where Mollie lived. Colonel Patton's wartime accomplishments that began at Scary Creek and ended at Winchester were probably never fully realized until many years later. It was then the impressive legacy he had left as a daring and courageous officer inspired his grandson, George S. Patton, III, to seek a military career.

Acknowledgments and Picture Credits

THIS BOOK WOULD NOT HAVE BEEN POSSIBLE WITHOUT THE undaunted spirit and dedication of the remarkable Hansford family and their descendants. To all of the family members, past and present, who recorded, preserved, and shared this invaluable segment of our grassroot history, a sincere expression of gratitude is extended.

In particular, those who deserve special recognition include: Mary Sue Woodson of Nitro, West Virginia, for her persistent research and labor in collecting most of the Hansford material; Russell L. Hansford of Marmet, West Virginia, for his assistance in locating family records and photos; also the various descendants of Maria (Teays) Barker, now residing in the Houston, Texas, area, for their willingness to share treasured family papers.

Other friends and associates who provided valuable information and support include: the late Robert Chapman of Huntington, West Virginia, for donating important Hansford letters from his personal Civil War collection; a special note of appreciation is extended to Mildred Lee Grove of Stephen City, Virginia, for graciously sharing her vast knowledge of the area and the times that Mollie Walls wrote about.

To my good friends Tom Denny and Terry Lowry for their proofreading chores and helpful suggestions, I am grateful.

A special thanks to Frederick Armstrong and Carol Vandevender and the other staff members of the West Virginia Division of Archives and History for their always friendly and cooperative assistance. Thanks are also extended to our long-time friends Dennis and Madeline Deitz for

sharing their experience and know-how in the publishing business.

Then, there are also those special friends and associates who share a common interest in Civil War history. They could always be counted on to furnish detailed information and suggestions, and their inspiration and encouragement along the way has been greatly appreciated. They include Richard Andre, Mort Doyle, Joe Ferrell, Terry Lowry, Okey Miller, Tim McKinney and Noble Wyatt.

Most of all I am grateful to my wife Ruth who patiently typed and retyped the manuscript. Although she is not necessarily historically motivated, she managed to remain tolerant and supportive throughout the long ordeal.

The photographs and drawings in this book are from a variety of sources which are credited as follows:

AC—Author's Collection
HFC—Hansford Family Collection
HFNHD—Harpers Ferry National Historic Park
JD—Jack Dickinson Collection, Huntington, W.Va.
LC—Library of Congress, Washington, D.C.
NA—National Archives
PM—Paul Marshall Collection, Charleston, W.Va.
SC—Stan Cohen Collection
VSA—Virginia State Archives
WFCHS—Winchester-Frederick County Historical Society
WVA—West Virginia State Archives, Charleston, W.Va.
WVU—West Virginia University Archives, Morgantown, W.Va.

Mollie Hansford Walls Rust (1828-1900) with grandsons Kenneth Schultz and Hugo Walls. HFC

DEDICATED
TO
MY GRANDCHILDREN
BRYAN, JOHNA, KALEENA AND JUANITA
THAT THEY MAY BETTER
APPRECIATE THEIR AMERICAN HERITAGE

Prologue

MOLLIE AND VICTORIA HANSFORD WERE BOTH BORN AT THE mouth of Paint Creek in the Kanawha Valley. When Mollie was six months old, her mother, Elizabeth Teays Hansford, died leaving her in the care of relatives. When she was three, her father, John Hansford, married Maria Morris who became Victoria's mother. She also had three other children, Charles, Carroll, and Cynthia. In 1840 the Hansfords, with their slaves, moved to Coalsmouth on a flatboat. The next year Maria Hansford died, leaving five motherless children. With the help of relatives and the family slaves, their father, John Hansford, managed to maintain the household and provide a happy, normal home life for the children.

Mollie grew up in Coalsmouth which was her home until 1853 when she married Dr. John W. Walls and went to live at Newtown (now Stephen City), near Winchester, Virginia. Dr. Walls had already established his home and practice at Newtown. He had been a widower with two children, William who was 15 and Mary who was just three. William was attending the Academy in Winchester and only came home on weekends, while Mary was cared for by a born-free Mulatto woman who had been her nursemaid since she was born. There were also four family slaves, so Mollie had plenty of time to manage the household, visit with her neighbors and keep up on the local news. As the clouds of war began to gather, she soon became caught up in the excitement of the times. Long before the first shot was fired, she had already become an uncompromising Rebel, which later led to several dangerous encounters with Federal soldiers.

Newtown, Virginia, was founded about 1758 by Lewis Stephens and was first called Stephensburg. It was located in the Shenandoah Valley, seven miles south of Winchester. It was situated on the Old Indian Road, which later became the Great Wagon Road that extended southwest through the Cumberland Gap into Kentucky and Tennessee. Long before the Civil War, the town became known for its flourishing wagon-making industry. Sturdy wagons bearing the famous Newtown brand carried many of the early western pioneers all the way to California. Between 1835 and 1840 the road through Newtown was macadamized from Winchester to Staunton and became known as the Valley Pike, which is now U.S. Route 11.

At the beginning of the war, Mollie Walls' front steps were only a few feet from this important highway. The Valley Pike was a prime objective of both armies all through the war. It was vital for moving troops and supplies, and whichever force controlled it maintained a strategic advantage.

Winchester, the gateway to the Shenandoah Valley, is said to have changed hands approximately 72 times during the war. Almost daily, opposing forces would clash somewhere along the hotly contested Pike, often in the neighborhood of Newtown. Usually these encounters were no more than hit-and-run skirmishes. There were, however, at least eight important battles fought within a 12-mile radius of Mollie's home. They included such epic struggles as the three battles of Winchester, two battles at Kernstown, Fisher's Hill, Front Royal, and Cedar Creek. In all, they accounted for over 30,000 American casualties. (See Appendix A for casualty totals.)

Often after a hard-fought battle, the outcome left one army in full retreat and the opposing force in hot pursuit. Many times when this occurred, overwhelming numbers of dead and wounded were left in the neighborhood for the civilians of the surrounding small towns and farms to care for the best they could. Since Mollie's husband was a civilian doctor, on numerous occasions they both went among the wounded doing what they could for the stricken men of both sides.

Stragglers and foragers were also a continual threat to civilians along the Pike, especially in the Newtown neighborhood. Since they were usually separated from their units, these wandering soldiers mostly foraged on their own, away from military control. Yankee stragglers were particularly dangerous, as many felt justified in harassing Rebels by taking food and often personal property from them. Since Dr. Walls was away from home much of the time, Mollie soon learned to stand her ground against all intruders in a defiant effort to protect her family and property. Since her first child, Hansford, was born during the first year of the war, his welfare and safety was always her foremost concern, no matter what crisis came her way.

There was yet another reason why Union troops harassed the Walls family more than their neighbors. Mollie's stepson William had become an army surgeon after finishing at Winchester Medical College in 1861. This was the same school that Federal forces had burned when it was rumored that the body of John Brown's son was used there as a cadaver, after he was killed at Harpers Ferry. Major William Walls was a surgeon in Stonewall Jackson's Brigade and assisted in removing the General's arm after he was wounded. Since he was well known in the area, local Yankee ranger units were always searching the Walls household hoping to catch him at home.

Although the Walls family miraculously came through the war unscathed, they, like many of their neighbors, were left practically destitute with no quick way to recover. Two of their former slaves chose to stay on with them at a meager wage, but Dr. Walls eventually had to send them to their families when he could no longer afford to pay and feed them.

The site of Coalsmouth in the Kanawha Valley was the first mentioned by James Hanson, a scribe who was there in 1774. He kept a journal for a surveying crew running off a land grant for George Washington. The grant included the site of present-day St. Albans.

In 1786 Lewis and Samuel Tackett built a fort a mile below the mouth of Coal. Tackett's Fort was attacked by Indians in 1789, and most of the occupants were either killed or captured. In 1800 Stephen Teays, Mollie's grandfather, became the first permanent settler on the lower side of the river. He also established a ferry and maintained an inn.

The James River and Kanawha Turnpike was completed in 1831 and ran from Richmond to Kentucky. The same year, James Teays built an inn, a stagecoach stop, and a toll bridge where the turnpike crossed Coal River.

The Coal River was made navigable in 1848 by the construction of a series of locks and dams. Cannel coal mined in Boone County was shipped down the river in barges. William S. Rosecrans, who later became a Union general, was president of the Coal River Navigation Company before the war. In 1861 when General Henry Wise left the valley, he scuttled all the loaded barges tied up at Coalsmouth's Lock No. 1. He also ordered the covered bridge burned that was located where the Main Street bridge now stands.

At the beginning of the war, Camp Tompkins was established a mile below town as a Confederate marshalling area and training center. The troops stationed there under the command of Captain George S. Patton received their baptism under fire at nearby Scary Creek. It was there that they managed to temporarily stop a superior Union force advancing up the Kanawha Valley.

Later, after the Federal Army gained control of the valley, they maintained a sizeable detachment at Coalsmouth throughout most of the war. Since a majority of the townspeople were pro-Confederate, the entire community was put under martial law, which imposed a great hardship on the citizens.

After Mollie married and left Coalsmouth, Victoria took over running the household, and by the time the war started, she had become a reliable and resourceful young lady. To help with the war effort, she organized and directed various activities to support and entertain Confederate troops who were in training at nearby Camp Tompkins. Later she encouraged the young people in her neighborhood to write letters and make up boxes to send to local soldiers who were held in northern prison camps.

Victoria Hansford took the time to record a great deal of what she saw and heard during the war. She wrote about the early assembly and training of militia units at nearby Camp Tompkins. She gave a first-hand report on how the Battle of Scary affected Coalsmouth and described the Great Flood of 1861. She also told about the triumphant return of the Rebel Army after Lightburn's retreat. In addition, Victoria left a first-hand account of how the people of Coalsmouth learned to manage under the military rule and harassment of Union occupation.

Neither Mollie nor Victoria had any intentions of documenting a military history of their part of the war. They simply wanted to leave a record of their own personal experiences and first-hand knowledge of the great conflict. Their writings have provided a rare picture of what life was really like for the many non-combatants who were caught in the crossfire.

In editing their original manuscripts, italicized notes were added to contribute to the scope and meaning of the narrative. The following chapters, however, are basically the original thoughts and words of the Hansford sisters.

CHAPTER ONE
THE BRIDAL TOUR

I WAS MARRIED JULY 31, 1853, AT OUR HOME IN Coalsmouth (now St. Albans, West Virginia). Dr. Walls had come on, several days before, that he might make all necessary preparations for our journey. He had gone to Charleston and hired a carriage and a driver to take us as far as White Sulphur Springs in Greenbrier County. From there we planned to take the stage. I had sent a servant around to ask all my aunts, uncles and cousins to come at nine o'clock the next morning for the wedding.

They were all there that could come and the older ladies thought it dreadful for me to marry and go so far away. They said I would not live a year as I was so delicate, and during the ceremony they all kept crying. Of course that made me feel dreadful but I only gave way for a minute and was laughing when I went upstairs to change for traveling.

When I came back down, the buggy was at the front gate looking very stylish with its pretty white trimmings, white horses and a black driver. I bade them all farewell as cheerful as I could, while feeling very sad, but not showing it. I had such perfect confidence in Dr. Walls that I felt it would be my own fault if I was not happy. All the servants crowded about me asking if I was going to take any of them with me. I told Jane that I could never think of taking her when her husband could not go. Besides, Dr. Walls had servants enough.

We went on to Charleston for dinner but stayed all night at Malden. The next morning was the first of August and we got an early start. The first place we stopped was at Uncle Morris Hansford's as he kept the toll gate on the road opposite the mouth of Paint Creek. When he came out to get our toll and saw me he was so surprised he hardly knew what to say. I introduced him to Dr. Walls and he wanted us to come in but we had to be on our way.

We made it to Gauley Bridge that evening where we stayed all night. I remember the place was not at all nice and we started very early the next morning. That night we

Typical style of the 1850s.

stayed at Tyree's Tavern, high in the mountains. It was an old place but well kept.

As neither Doctor nor myself knew anything about the roads, we depended on the old black driver to know the way and to stop where he thought best. We soon discovered he was looking out for places where the horses could get good feed more than he was concerned about us.

Our next stop was at Blue Sulphur Springs which was a pretty place and there were a great many people there from Kanawha. At that time it was a favorite resort of the Charleston folks as scarcely any of them went on to White Sulphur. From there we went on to Lewisburg and put up at Stonaker's Hotel and stayed over Sunday as Doctor would not travel on Sundays. That was a nice place and we went to church and rested the remainder of the day.

Monday morning we went on to White Sulphur which was only 10 miles. Mr. Truslow who we had hired the buggy from had followed us up with other passengers to the White. He was driving a fine buggy with two beautiful dark gray horses, they were twin colts. He tried

Tyree's Tavern or Halfway House at Ansted, Fayette County, on old Route 60. It was built in 1810 and used as the headquarters of the Chicago Grey Dragoons during the winter of 1861-62. Still standing 1989.

Blue Sulphur Springs in 1859. Just prior to the war this famous health resort was turned into a Baptist College. During the war, the spa was used by both armies as a hospital. In the winter of 1862-63, several hundred Georgia troops were encamped here. Eighty-nine of them died of a typhoid fever epidemic and were buried on top of the hill in coffins made out of benches from the cottages and buildings of the resort. In 1864, Union troops burned down the rest of the buildings.
VSA

to get Dr. Walls to buy them to take us on home. We had planned to give up our buggy at Lewisburg or White Sulphur and take a stage the rest of the way, however, we found all out-going stages were already full.

We put up at Frazier's Hotel on the hill above the springs and we stayed there several days trying to get on the stage. Miss Sara Frazier found out that I was a Hansford and she came to our room to see me. She was a niece of my Uncle Felix and Aunt Sara (Frazier) Hansford. She invited us to go to the ballroom with her to watch some of the fashionable bells and their escorts dance.

There was a great crowd there that year from all of the large cities. Jerome Bonaparte, his wife and child were there from Baltimore. I tell you they put on the style, he looked very much like pictures of his Uncle Napoleon Bonaparte. His wife was a fine looking lady. She rode out on horseback with him wearing a black velvet riding habit with diamond buttons up the front. Their child rode in an open carriage with a nurse and a Negro driver.

The Bonaparte that Mollie Walls saw at White Sulphur Springs was Jerome Napoleon, the son of Napoleon's brother, Jerome, and Elizabeth Patterson.

In 1803 while serving with the French Navy, Jerome Bonaparte, Napoleon's brother, visited the United States and married Elizabeth Patterson of Baltimore, without the consent of his family. After living in Baltimore for two years, Captain Bonaparte and his wife sailed for Europe in 1805. On reaching Lisbon, a French frigate was there to prevent her from landing. Jerome left his wife and went to Paris to plead her cause with the Emperor, while the ship proceeded to Amsterdam. At the entrance to the harbor, two French warships barred the way, and Elizabeth Bonaparte was forced to seek asylum in England.

A few days after arrival in England, her son, Jerome Napoleon Bonaparte, was born. There she remained awaiting the resolution of her marriage. Napoleon applied to Pope Pius VII to dissolve the marriage, but the Pontiff steadfastly refused. A decree of divorce was then passed by the Imperial Council of State. A lifetime pension of 60,000 francs a year was granted to Elizabeth and her son, and they returned to Baltimore.

The father married Princess Catherine of Wurtemberg in 1807 and became king of Westphalia. The son graduated at Harvard in 1826 and married Miss Williams of Roxbury, Massachusetts. Through his inheritances, Jerome Napoleon Bonaparte became one of the richest men in Baltimore, where he died in 1870. — Appletons' Cyclopedia of American Biography.

When we went to the ballroom with Miss Frazier she was dressed in white with a great deal of trimmings. She wore a gold chain, earrings, bracelets, and her fingers were crowded with rings. Her hair was curled with flowers and I thought her over dressed. I determined to look as plain as possible. I wore a dotted swiss, made with an infant waist, a white sash and a few white flowers at my waist. I had a white fanion on my head, with my hair crimped in front and combed back plain as they wear it now. I wore no jewelry but my wedding rings.

After we were all in the ballroom a short time, Bettie Burns came up to me. She was the same light-hearted Bettie I had known before and she seemed so glad to see me. She introduced me to her sister Mrs. Caldwell, whose husband was part owner of the White at that time. Sarah Frazier was a cousin of Bettie's and she afterwards married a Mr. Summerson who was a stage agent at Staunton, Virginia.

Mrs. Caldwell was the wife of William Caldwell who at that time was part owner of the resort. He had inherited his interest from his father, James Caldwell, who has been referred to as the "Father of White Sulphur Springs."

James Caldwell was a sea merchant who came from Baltimore to the White Sulphur area in 1795. He married a daughter of Michael Boyer who owned the land that included the Springs. In 1816 James Caldwell became sole proprietor of the property and began the development of the White Sulphur Springs. — The White Sulphur Springs by William A. MacCorkle.

There still seemed no prospect of leaving as the stages were always crowded. The hotels were so filled up that some of the incoming passengers slept in the stages during the night with the promise of a room the next day. We found Mr. Truslow had not yet left and he still wanted to sell the horses and buggy for $500.00. After Dr. Walls had again looked them over he decided to buy them but he had not that much money with him. However, I was able to make up the difference by giving Mr. Truslow a check on the Kanawha Bank where I had my money.

The next morning a number of our friends, new and old, were out to see us off. The horses looked so beautiful, however, it took two men to hold them while we got in. I never thought of danger, but there really was none for after we drove several miles they began to quiet down. We later discovered they had been hitched up the wrong way as they had been trained one for the right side and one for the left.

After leaving the White we traveled slowly, stopping at noon to feed our horses and eat our lunch which we always had packed where we had stayed the night before.

The weather was delightful and I never enjoyed anything as much as that luncheon beside a cool spring high in the mountains. We were passing over the Alleghanies and the scenery was lovely.

We next stopped to rest at Hot Springs, the hotel was on the side of the mountain and the bath houses were below, near the springs. There were very few people there except invalids. We next stopped at the Warm Springs and then continued on to Bath Alum which was also a beautiful place.

After we reached Staunton, we got on the macadamized pike that led up the Shenandoah Valley. It was at that time the best road I ever saw, smooth and as solid as a floor. I tell you with our two fast horses and light buggy we really traveled fast. We had put all our baggage on the stage except one small trunk, my band box and Doctor's case.

The turnpike was to be constructed from Winchester to Harrisonburg (later to Staunton) under the Charter of 1834. It was to be 22 feet wide, 18 feet paved or macadamized not less than 12 inches thick. The company was to construct the turnpike along or on the site of the existing stage road, passing through Union Mills, Kernstown, Newtown (now Stephen City), and Middletown, and no grade was to exceed three degrees. It is probable the road was not completed much before 1840. The fact that the road could be built in five or six years was surprising when you remember that the breaking of stones for a foot-thick bed had to be done by hand. — Twenty-Five Chapters on the Shenandoah Valley by John W. Wayland.

After we neared New Market we stopped for the night at a place of entertainment called the "Flowering Springs." It was an old place kept by an old couple named Lincoln. We later determined that they were related to the Ruffners in Charleston. Everything was so plain and neat with the cleanest and freshest beds. I could hardly make the old lady believe I was Dr. Walls' wife, she thought I was his daughter. She was so kind, she made a bright wood fire in my room to dry out my things as we had been driving in the rain all day. She also had the best supper, fried chicken, batter cakes, the nicest honey and all kinds of other good things I can't remember. I was hungry and ate more than usual.

From Mollie's description, they stayed all night at one of the most celebrated old taverns on the Valley Pike. It was Lincoln Inn, at Lacey Spring, formerly known as Big Spring. The structure was a log house, two stories high, a landmark in the Valley since colonial times.

In 1833 David Lincoln became the proprietor of the old inn, and the same year in Sagamon County, Illinois, his cousin Abraham Lincoln was also granted license to keep a tavern. David Lincoln died in 1849 and his widow, Catherine, continued to run the business. The old tavern remained until 1898 when it was destroyed by fire. — Twenty-Five Chapters on Shenandoah Valley by John Wayland.

The next morning when we left it was bright and the country along the way was beautiful, such large farms, with stone walls on each side of the Pike all the way. We

The Valley Pike. WFCHS

drove fast as we wanted to reach Mt. Jackson where we intended to stay all night with a friend of Doctor's, a Dr. Jordan. Long before we got there it began raining again and we drove very fast. When we arrived at the house I ran in dripping wet. Doctor went to get my trunk, and lo! we had lost it off the back of the buggy. Dr. Jordan proposed to send someone back to look along the road as there were very few houses. Doctor, however, decided that he should go himself, and he had not gone far until he met a colored man coming with it. The man had been working in a nearby field when he saw the trunk fall off. He went immediately to his master and got permission to pick it up and follow us on a horse. We were so glad to get it and Doctor paid him well. It was so honest and thoughtful of him, most servants would not have done as he did. Dr. Jordan and his family were very kind and pleasant, one of his daughters visited us afterwards.

We expected to get home that day but we did not arrive until almost sundown. Doctor's house was the last one at the northeast end of town. Therefore, we had to drive about a mile down the main street in the evening while most people were sitting on their front porches. Everyone knew Dr. Walls but they did not expect to see him coming home with a new wife and a new buggy. As we drove by they all waved and looked after us until we were out of sight.

As the last stage had already passed, his folks had about given us up. Only his sister Bettie and the cook Mary were there to receive me. Mary was full of fun and said she had told Miss Bettie we would be home that evening as she had read it in the grounds left in her coffee cup. They almost carried me in the house and they soon had a nice supper on the table. All the servants seemed so kind. I was so tired that night and I soon retired. Mine was a large room with three full-length windows, two facing east and one looking south. It was a cheerful and healthy looking room that was beautifully furnished. It had a large bedstead with lemon colored curtains around it. There was also another smaller bed, more fashionable, made all in white. There was a beautiful white china chamber set, a nice dressing case and an ingrain carpet. The curtains were white muslin, and there were two vases and a lamp on the mantle. Lamps were not generally used at that time, therefore, it looked pretty to me. Back home we used candles and lard oil lamps. The oil we use now was not known then.

CHAPTER TWO
ANTE-BELLUM YEARS

THE NEXT MORNING BETTIE SHOWED ME ALL THROUGH THE house. It was built with large, square-frame timbers filled in with brick, making it very strong. It had an ell with a long porch running the full length of the house. There was a wide hall running between the main house and the ell, with Venetian shutters at the ends instead of doors.

The Walls' house as described was built using the old half-timber method of construction. The house was framed with massive exposed hewed beams with corner posts, studs and cross-bracing. The open spaces were filled in with nogging which was usually brick laid in courses.

They opened into a flower garden surrounded by rare trees and shrubbery. The ell contained the kitchen and the cook's room. There was a high board fence between the garden and kitchen yard that was almost completely covered with running roses. There were beds of annuals of all kinds in the center of the garden. Everything was beautiful.

Cousin Bettie, as I called Doctor's sister, was full of life and a great talker. As she was showing me around she would ask every few minutes how I liked my new home. The dining room was just to my notion, it had two large windows looking east. I always liked sunlight in a dining

HALF-TIMBER HOUSE

room in the morning. It makes everything so cheerful. It had a fireplace in one corner, a door into the hall and another door into the doctor's office. There was a round table in the middle sitting on a white drugget with bunches of roses woven in it. A "crumb cloth" of white linen was also kept under the table. There was a large beautiful mahogany sideboard that was said to have cost 60 dollars. A quantity of fine glass and silverware were kept here, and also two large pewter pitchers were always there. They were very old and had been in the family a long time. Everything on the sideboard was kept shiny by a small Negrillo servant. Although he was 79, he was only the size of a boy. It was his job to keep everything pertaining to the dining room in perfect order.

The hallway was wide and the walls were covered with black and white oil cloth. There was a pretty stairway covered with fine carpet held down with shiny brass rods. At the head of the stairs was a store room with shelves from the floor to the ceiling on both sides. They were stowed full of all kinds of dried and preserved fruit, pickles and honey. We had no canned fruit or vegetables then. There were several four-gallon jars full of dried cherries packed in sugar. I had never seen them before and I liked them better than raisins. I used to keep my apron pockets full all the time. Oh! they were good.

There were two other bedrooms upstairs besides ours. The parlor was a very large handsome room with an open wood fireplace that had high brass andirons and a brass fender. There was a pretty mantle piece with beautiful lamps and two china vases. There was a large

window on each side of the fireplace that looked out on the flower garden. The windows had blue curtains trimmed with blue and gold fringe. The furniture and carpet were almost new.

Doctor had two children, William who was 15, the son of his first wife, and there was also Mary Octavia, who was three years old. Her mother was his second wife who had died at Mary's birth. She was from Washington, D.C., a beautiful, high-educated woman but she only lived five years after they were married. Mary was a sweet child with very pretty brown hair. Doctor had hired a Mulatto nurse who was born free to tend to her altogether after her mother died. She was as refined and as nice in manners as any white lady. Her name was Cornelia Fletcher and Mary was very fond of her. After the war started, Doctor sent Cornelia and Mary to Washington to live with her mother's people as he thought she would be safer there.

William's mother was a Miss Littler from Capon Springs in Hampshire County. She was of an admirable sweet disposition but was delicate and died with consumption when William was but six years old.

When I married Dr. Walls, his two maiden sisters were living at the old home place in Winchester where they were born and raised. It was a sweet old place on the corner of Braddock and Clifford Streets located on a one-acre lot and was surrounded by an old-fashioned flower garden, rare shrubbery and a variety of fruit trees.

William boarded with them while he attended the Academy and he was their pet and idol. He generally walked home every Friday and back on Sunday. He had a beautiful dog named Rover, a large black and white New Foundland that he was very fond of. He spent much of his time while home with his dog, hunting and teaching him new tricks. William could give him a basket and send him to the post office a half mile away and he would always bring the mail back safe. He generally ran along beside our carriage and when we got where we were going he would jump up in the seat and would let no strangers come near.

One day I went to Winchester to purchase some things for a church festival the ladies were going to have. I had the money in my pocketbook which I put in a small basket behind the seat. When we got to town we found the basket had bounced out of the buggy some place back along the road. Just as we started back to look for it, Rover came into view with the basket in his mouth.

When William left for the Army in 61, it was as hard for him to part with Rover as it was to say good bye to the family. One day during the war, Rover was in front of our door when a Yankee soldier tried to get in. When he saw he could not get past the dog, he ran his bayonet through his shoulder. We did all we could for his wound but it would not heal. He lingered for months and finally one morning we found him dead on the door step. As our colored boy Henry said, "We buried him in the garden with honors."

CHAPTER THREE
MOLLIE GOES TO JOHN BROWN'S TRIAL

IT WAS A COMFORTABLE, EASY WAY OF LIFE THAT MOLLIE *Hansford Walls and her family settled into during those ante-bellum years from 1853 to 1861. However, after John Brown's raid at nearby Harpers Ferry, the threatening clouds of war began to cast a shadow over their peaceful household. By then, Mollie and her husband were already becoming caught up in the controversial issues of the day. They had even gone to Charles Town for the John Brown trials which seemed to be the fashionable and patriotic thing to do at the time. She wrote the following letter to her brother Carroll back in Coalsmouth describing what it was like in Charles*

Town two days before Brown was hanged.

Carroll Hansford was already training with the Kanawha Riflemen, a militia company under Captain George S. Patton. (Captain Patton was the grandfather of General George S. Patton III of World War II fame.) The company was made up of young men from the more prominent families of the area. They later became Company H of the 22nd Virginia Volunteers.

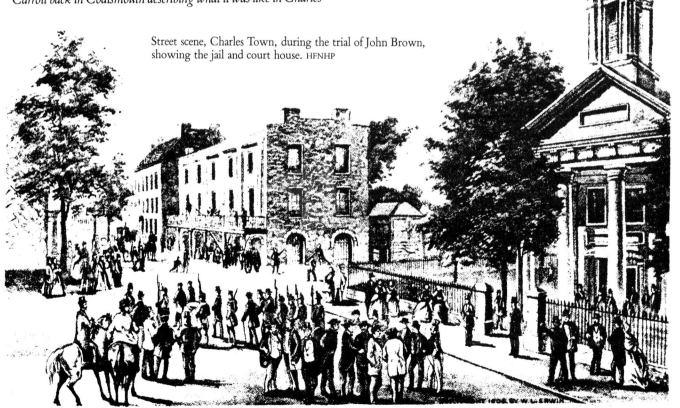

Street scene, Charles Town, during the trial of John Brown, showing the jail and court house. HFNHP

Newtown

Dec. 1st, 1859

Dear Brother:

Well, as none of you will write to me I must to you. I have not received a letter for three weeks—what is the matter? If you had as much to keep you from writing as I have, you might talk. We are kept in a continual state of excitement day and night. Men are marching and drums are beating by our house all the time. There are continual reports of all kinds that keep the people frightened to death.

If you were here and had seen and heard as much as I have you would have no mercy on Brown and his gang. I suppose you think you hear enough of this in the papers without me writing about it, but there is nothing else talked of here. We scarcely do any work for running to the door every few minutes to see companies of soldiers and wagon loads of supplies go by.

Dr. and I went to Charles Town and stayed two days during the end of Brown's trial, we just got home last evening after dark. Oh, I wish you could have seen what we saw, I never expect to see such a beautiful, yet awesome, sight. There were 3,000 regular troops on parade at once. Every company dressed in different colored uniforms. There were three companies of the Richmond Grays with uniforms of gray trimmed with white, all with splendid new guns and bayonets. A company from Wheeling was dressed in green, trimmed with gold braid; they were a beautiful sight. The West Augusta Guards from Staunton were dressed in dark blue, trimmed with gilt braid and they wore tall caps with blue plumes. A company from Petersburg wore dark gray with bright yellow caps and trim. There was a group from Norfolk that wore gray uniforms trimmed in bright red. There was also another company dressed in light blue uniforms. There is no use to try to tell you how they all looked for it is impossible.

The Lexington Cadets (VMI) were also there and were camped just below the garden where we were staying. Their drums woke us up at daylight every morning. Indeed we could sleep but little for the hollering of the sentinels every half hour all over town.

There have been so many fires set around Charles Town by abolitionists that a cavalry troop patrols the countryside day and night. One cavalry unit is from Newtown—50 well-mounted soldiers as handsome and well dressed as any company here. You remember John Chipley, our neighbor, he is a sergeant in the company and he looks very handsome in his uniform. Tip Chipley, his brother, is also with them but he is unable to walk. He was in a house one night that was set fire and he had to jump out a window and he sprained his ankle.

There are sentinels stationed all around town, no one can get in or out unless they know a password. Anyone living on the edge of town cannot get to the courthouse square. We tried to go from Mr. North's to Mr. Hunter's on Front Street but every way we turned we were stopped. We were halted by a sentinel with a bayonet on his gun and he called out, "Halt, you can't pass." By then there were about 20 of us and we had to stay where we were as now there was a sentinel on every corner. Some of the group got mad and some were frightened while others laughed about it. Finally, a man with us went to headquarters and got permission from the officer of the guard to let us all pass. We were almost late getting out to the cars (trains) to come home. We would not have made it if the train had not been held up while they searched it.

They have only been this strict during the last two days as two men were seen in the area thought to be related to Edwin Coppock, one of the prisoners. I saw all the important men and had introductions to some of them, such as the U.S. Marshal Jennings Wise. I also saw his father Governor Henry Wise. He was a little man, white headed, looks as fierce as a lizard. All the great editors were there, there were two of them where we stayed. The courthouse was full of soldiers, as were all the schoolhouses, storehouses, shops, and even all the empty houses in town were full.

It was warm as summertime, we sat with the door open and walked about without any shawls. It was the most beautiful weather I ever saw for this time of the year. It seemed like everything and everybody except abolitionists were smiling on "Old Brown's" execution. No one can feel any sympathy for him after they see the dreadful instruments he had prepared to kill us with. I had one of the spikes in my hand and examined it, the pictures you see in the papers are exactly like them. They are made rough and course, they were for the Negroes to use. The guns were the most complete things you ever saw, they were not loaded with bullets but fired slugs.

He was not the least cowed or sorry but says the only thing he regrets is letting the cars pass that night. He always had hopes of being saved until yesterday when they took him to the front window to look out at the troops and cannons in front of the jail. He turned away and said it was no use to hope now as his friends could not rescue him. He said he thought it would be better for him to die now as there would be thousands to rise up in his place to avenge him. Oh, he is a dreadful man, may the Lord have mercy on him for man cannot.

I have filled my letter with Brown and his doings. Do write when you have time. Tell Father that Doctor is very impatient to hear from him. Tell Cint, Vic, and Charley to write. We are all well and hope you are.

As ever your affectionate sister,
M.J. Walls

Brown was executed at 11:30 a.m. on Dec. 2, 1859, in a field just outside Charles Town, Jefferson County. HFNHP

CHAPTER FOUR
THE WAR COMES TO COALSMOUTH

MOLLIE'S FAMILY BACK HOME IN COALSMOUTH (NOW ST. Albans, West Virginia) had also become deeply involved in the local war effort. Her sister Victoria Hansford, who was 23 at the time, had become a rousing supporter for the Rebel cause. Realizing that each day important history was being made around Coalsmouth, she felt a responsibility to record much of what she saw and heard. Her journals on the Civil War in Coalsmouth have been preserved, and most of her writings are included in this work.

Her father, John Hansford, although deeply concerned about the state of affairs, had little time to take an active part in the local war effort. His essential community duties as postmaster and magistrate kept him fully occupied together with his other duties of keeping an inn, manning a stage coach stop, and collecting toll on the covered bridge.

Brother Charley Hansford had been teaching school at the Mill Road School, which later became Fairview School. At the first alert of a possible invasion of the Kanawha Valley by Union Forces, the school was closed for the duration.

Sister Cynthia was 21 in 1861 and had gone to stay with Mollie at Newtown to help her with the new baby.

Brother Carroll "Kit" Hansford had already joined the Kanawha Riflemen under Captain George Patton and was stationed at Camp Tompkins, only a mile from the Hansford home place at Coalsmouth. Victoria described the situation at Coalsmouth as she recorded it in her "Reminiscents of the War—1861."

WINTZ

The Teays Inn and Toll Gate on the bridge at Coalsmouth as it was before the War.

The spring of 1861 came as all other springs with its sunshine, its birds, and it flowers, yet we hailed it not with the usual joy and anticipation. Far away we could hear the rumblings of the storm that we feared would soon sweep over our beautiful valley. Fort Sumter had already fallen, there had been blood shed in Maryland, and now there had been a great stir in Western Virginia.

Mr. George Patton from Charleston had heretofore been a staunch Union man and had previously made stirring speeches in our town in favor of the Union. Recently, however, he returned speaking eloquently and calling on all sons of Virginia to rally around her flag. He was cheered lustily and how patriotic we felt as we waved our handkerchiefs. We all sang "We Will Die for Old Virginia." Altogether, this was an exciting day in our quiet little village of Coalsmouth.

Nine of our young men volunteered in Captain Patton's Company known as the Kanawha Riflemen. They were my brother Carroll Hansford, Stephen Teays, N.B. Brooks, Charlie Turner, Theodore Turner, Thornton Thompson, Tom Grant, James Rust, and Henry Gregory. The citizens of Coalsmouth gathered around the wagon to tell them good bye and to wish them "God speed." Tears were not only shed by their mothers and sisters, but many others there that day wept over the sacrifices they were about to make.

Colonel George S. Patton, grandfather of General George S. Patton of World War II fame. WVA

The concerns and anxieties of those who were there that day were justified, since six of the nine men who left would die in service, and the other three would be captured and left to suffer in northern prison camps. The Turner brothers, Charlie and Theodore, both died a day apart near Princeton with typhoid fever, and Thornton Thompson died several days later at the same place. Tom Grant died in prison at Pt. Lookout, Maryland, after being captured at Cold Harbor. He was the son of Roswel Grant of Coalsmouth who was an uncle of General Ulysses S. Grant. Carroll Hansford, N.B. Brooks, and Stephen Teays were all captured and held in northern prisons. James Rust and his brother-in-law, Henry Gregory, both died in battle.

As early as May 1861, Camp Tompkins was established a mile below Coal River, not far from where the Hansfords lived. It was a Confederate assembly and training center for the lower Kanawha Valley area. By early July, just before the Battle of Scary, approximately 3,000 troops had been assembled there. By then it was known that General Jacob D. Cox had gathered a Federal force across the Ohio and was prepared to launch an invasion of the Kanawha Valley. Victoria described some of the activity that took place in her neighborhood during those exciting days.

A camp had been established about two miles below Charleston by Captain George Patton of the Kanawha Riflemen, Captain John Swann of the Charleston Sharpshooters and Captain Andrew Barbee of the Border Rifles. These companies I believe were among the first that went into camp in western Virginia. They remained there until May when they were called to Buffalo about 25 miles below here. While they were there in camp, I went down to see "our boys" as did many others, thinking they might soon be sent far away. I stayed at Mrs. Wyatt's and had a pleasant visit. But then when it was determined that Buffalo might be attacked, we turned our faces homeward with many misgivings as to the future welfare of our dear ones. Sure that Buffalo would be attacked, Colonel Mc-Causland ordered the troops to withdraw back up the valley as it would be impossible to hold the position even against a small force.

Colonel John B. McCausland (1837-1927), who was in charge of the troops at Buffalo, later became a Brigade Commander and was promoted to Brigadier General. During the war, he gained recognition for burning Chambersburg, Pennsylvania, and for successfully defending Lynchburg, Virginia, from destruction by General David Hunter. Refusing to surrender at Appomattox, he led his troops safely through the lines. On reaching the vicinity of Lynchburg, he learned that Union stragglers were pil-

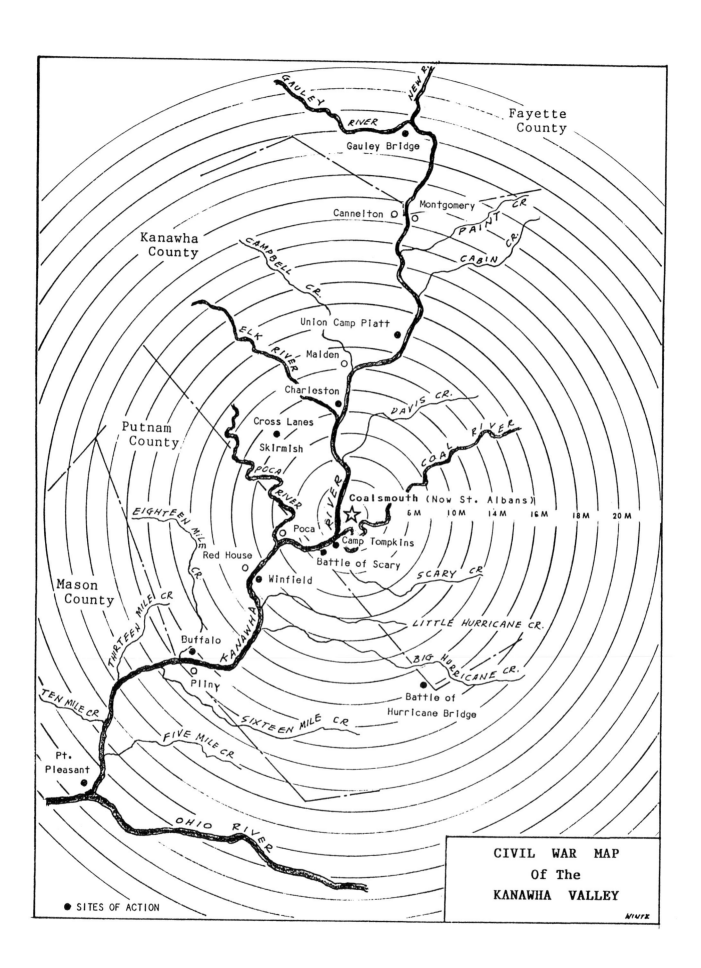

CIVIL WAR MAP
Of The
KANAWHA VALLEY

● SITES OF ACTION

fering and looting the city. Forming a skirmish line, his men swept through the town driving the Yankees before them, again coming to the rescue of the people of the city.

Several years after the war, the grateful citizens of Lynchburg invited General McCausland back and presented him with an engraved sword and a pair of silver spurs.

He eventually returned to the Kanawha Valley and built an impressive home that is still standing at Pliny in Mason County, just across the river from Buffalo. He live at Pliny until his death in 1927. (See Appendix D for roster of Buffalo Guards.)

Charlotte McCausland (1884-1971), the General's daughter holding sword that the grateful citizens of Lynchburg, Virginia, presented her father.

"Miss Charlotte" once told the writer about sitting on General Joseph E. Johnston's lap when as a small girl she attended the reunion of Confederate officers, with her father, held at White Sulphur Springs. AC

One day about sunset in early May, the steamboats "Julia Moffat" and "Kanawha Valley" came up the river with troops on board and landed below the mouth of Coal. We ladies had been molding bullets all day for the soldiers as there seemed to be a shortage.

As soon as we heard the boats had arrived, we all went down to welcome them. We all cheered and waved and their band responded by playing "Dixie" and some other pretty tunes from the boat. They then landed and marched to Camp Tompkins where they were soon joined by Captain Jenkin's company from Cabell County and other troops from Wayne and Boone counties. They were later formed into the 22nd Regiment under Colonel C.Q. Tompkins.

Then came those pleasant days like an oasis in a desert. The regiment was made up almost entirely of young men from Kanawha and adjoining counties. Our friends and relatives were all among them, and we went to and fro taking them things that would make their camp life more comfortable. We seemed to forget why they were there, and the threat of conflict seemed far away. Evening after evening we walked down to the camp to see them on dress parade and hear the music from the Kanawha Riflemen's brass band. They were well drilled, having excellent drill masters.

One morning about the last of June, I heard loud cheering down at the mouth of Coal River. I threw on my bonnet and ran in that direction as fast as I could to see what was going on. There I could see soldiers ascending

Both Armies used steamboats to transport troops on the Kanawha River.

the high hill across the Kanawha opposite the mouth of Coal. They were going in Indian file up the winding road and here and there through the openings in the trees could be seen different companies, each in their different uniforms. First were the Kanawha Riflemen under Captain Patton in their gray jackets, then came Captain Bailey's company in blue, and there was also Captain Barbee's company and Captain Lewis' cavalry. They all joined in singing "Virginia Boys" to the tune of Dixie. It sounded beautiful as the light breeze bore it down the mountain and across the river. Then when they sang "We Will Die for Old Virginia," it brought tears to our eyes.

They had been ordered to Riply by the most direct route to drive back several companies of Federal troops. They had crossed over from Ohio to plunder and harass secessionists who lived in the area. There was a skirmish with three of their men killed and several wounded while none of our men were injured. They were only gone a few days but soon after, several companies were sent back to Buffalo on steamboats. Some Union men at Pt. Pleasant, with the help of a few soldiers from Gallipolis, had arrested some prominent citizens. They were to be held as hostages for two Union men who had been taken by Captain Jenkins for disloyalty to the State. By the time our soldiers arrived, they found the Federal troops had returned to Ohio.

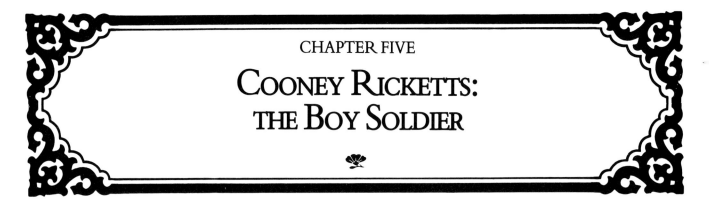

CHAPTER FIVE

COONEY RICKETTS: THE BOY SOLDIER

SOON AFTER, CAPTAIN ALBERT G. JENKINS ARRIVED AT CAMP Tompkins with his troop of Border Rangers from Green Bottom on the Ohio River. We ladies made and presented his company with a flag, it was a pretty one carefully made of the best material. Miss Sallie Lasley wrote our speech and her younger sister Allie delivered it. My father, John Hansford, held the flag unfurled to the breeze as it was presented to the company. They were all mounted and their horses were arranged in formation along the fence. They were under the shade of two locust trees that were in the yard of the old hotel near the covered bridge over Coal River. Captain Jenkins accepted it gracefully with a short and appropriate speech. We ladies stood on the lawn in front of the hotel with arms full of flowers in abundance which were showered over the officers and soldiers at the end of the ceremony.

Teays Tavern at Coalsmouth.

James D. Sedinger, one of the Ranger troopers who was there that day, wrote about it later in his "Diary of a Border Ranger." His description of the ceremony was the same as Victoria's account, except he was able to add more to the story. Sedinger recorded that when the nearby Battle of Scary was fought two months later, their flag was the only Confederate colors on the field.

Here I will relate an incident which occurred at the flag presentation ceremony which was very unusual for the times. When the flowers were being presented to the soldiers, one young lady having seen a small boy with the company, requested to present her bouquet to him. Captain Jenkins then called him up and he rode forward on a little mule with a rope bridle and no saddle. He wore a little cap and a very plain suit of everyday clothing. After he received his flowers, the captain introduced him as Lucian Ricketts. He said he had been adopted as a "child of the regiment" and then proceeded to tell us his story.

He said that when they were in camp at Greenbottom in Cabell County, this boy who was now only 14 years old had been drilling with them whenever he could borrow a horse. When they were ordered here to Camp Tompkins he went to his uncle's farm and appropriated this frisky little mule and began following the company. When I was told he was behind us I sent him word to return home, but he only dropped back and continued to tag along. Finding my orders disregarded, I rode to the rear and ordered him to go back home. I knew his mother, who was a widow and would surely be nearly deranged finding him gone. Another one of her sons, Albert Gallatin Ricketts, who is my namesake, is also in the company. When I began to reason with him he said "Captain, the road is free, I will ride in sight of you by day and camp nearby at night." When I told him he was too young for duty he said, "I can carry water, I can wait on you and do about anything, but I am determined to go to war." We could hold out no longer and that night we voted to adopt him as "The Child of the Regiment."

He went by the name of "Cooney" Ricketts and afterwards he always rode at the head of the column beside his beloved captain who was also very fond of him. The company was camped directly across from where I lived just below Tacketts Creek. They were in great need for pistols as they could get none through the army at that time. Captain Jenkins conceived a plan to obtain some which involved the service of young Cooney Ricketts. He was furnished with a good supply of money and was set off astride his little mule in the direction of Guyandotte. Arriving in

his home town he left his mule with relatives and boarded a steamer for Cincinnati. Arriving in the city, so as not to arouse suspicion, he began buying up pistols, one here and one there until he had obtained the required number. He then went out to the Union Camp Dennison where he collected important information regarding troop numbers and movements.

After his successful return with the guns, Cooney was nicely equipped with a new bridle and saddle for his mule. As he and the mule were both little, the ladies all thought him cute, sweet and brave. A great many tried to get him to return home, but all to no avail.

In less than six months after they left Coalsmouth, young Ricketts had become a full-fledged Border Ranger. When the 8th Cavalry raided Guyandotte the following November, relatives reported seeing him riding near the head of the attacking column. Since he was under age, he was never officially assigned nor carried on any rolls of the regiment. We do know he rode with the 8th Cavalry until August 22, 1863. It was on his 16th birthday that Captain Jenkins enrolled Cooney Ricketts at the Virginia Military Institute under the guardianship of a friend, Captain Waller R. Preston.

On May 16, 1864, when the VMI cadets were called out to take part in the Battle of New Market, Ricketts received special mention. He was acting as personal courier for General Scott Shipp, Commandant of the Corps of Cadets and was mounted on a horse. General John C. Breckinridge, commanding, gave the order for all officers to go into the charge dismounted. Not being an officer, Ricketts did not deem the order applied to him and he was the only one in the battle on horseback.

Colonel Francis L. Smith wrote later: "I would like to see some mention of 'Cooney' Ricketts for I thought he acted with great gallantry, riding ahead and in front of the corps when we became engaged with the enemy. I was put on his horse after being wounded and was taken back to New Market."

Less than a month after the battle, Union General David Hunter entered Lexington and burned the school. The cadets who had retreated to a camp in the Blue Ridge were furloughed and sent home. Cooney Ricketts, however, returned to his old company and was with them when they rode out of Appomattox avoiding surrender.

Lucian "Cooney" Ricketts returned to Cabell County where he studied law and was admitted to the bar in 1869. He was twice prosecuting attorney of Cabell County and was a Federal Land Examiner under the Cleveland administration. He died in 1906 and is buried in the Spring Hill Cemetery in Huntington, and his stone states simply Lucian C. Ricketts, VMI New Market Cadets, CSA, 1846-1906.

Cooney Ricketts.

General Hunter's wrath. The burned out remnants of VMI in 1864.

CHAPTER SIX

THE BATTLE OF SCARY: THREE MILES FROM COALSMOUTH

AT COALSMOUTH THE PLEASANT SUMMER DAYS OF JULY were passing and even though we were daily expecting the war to reach us we still managed to be cheerful. Our boys were yet at Camp Tompkins and the soil of Virginia up to now had not been invaded by the ruthless foe. However, a looming battle in our area was fast approaching.

My brothers would not hear to my remaining home any longer as I was already the only white female still in town. They directed that I should refugee to Paint Creek until after the battle. Ah, those were heart rending times. To go away and leave my father and two brothers behind with the enemy advancing slowly up the valley. I was to go on horseback but then Uncle Alva Hansford concluded to take me in his buggy.

Then came the question—what should I take and what should I leave. I could take very little and necessarily it was mostly clothing. All the things I prized so much had to be left and it was altogether likely I would never see the old home again or anything in it. The servants, six in

number, were sent a few miles up Coal River at the farm of Frank Thompson where his Negro quarters were. It was a sad parting—all of us going in different directions, my father and brothers into battle was the worst of all.

These were the times that tried women's hearts, but I had to be brave and strong, and never a tear did I shed. Had I been allowed to stay I would have done so but everyone had refugeed. A great many had gone to the Falls of Coal to be out of the way of the battle. Indeed, people went in all directions to get out of the village as it was thought the homes would be burned if the Yankees ever got this far since our soldiers were encamped here. My brother Charley gave me his money to keep for him. I made a hole in the ground and buried all of my mother's silver and some other valuable things.

So I left home the day before the Battle of Scary, which was fought on July 17, 1861. We started in the afternoon for Paint Creek and had to drive very hard to get there that night. The road was full of refugees going up the

An early view of the Felix G. Hansford house, still standing (1989) at the mouth of Paint Creek.

valley and from all directions soldiers and armed civilians were going down the valley towards the advancing foe. Weeping women and sad, unhappy children were all along the road. When I got to Paint Creek I found many others in the same fix as I was.

I went to my Uncle Felix Hansford's where they received us gladly and made us as comfortable as possible although the house was full. The girls were all put up in the office building in the yard above the road. What a merry time we had, we forgot for a while that the war clouds were hovering over us. The young are so full of life and hope.

The next day we heard the Battle of Scary had been fought with the loss of three of our men and six or eight on the Federal side. It was a hot fight that lasted all afternoon. We also took several prominent officers as prisoners. Captain Patton of the Kanawha Riflemen was wounded in the shoulder and a Yankee Colonel Neff was badly wounded. *(It was Colonel Jesse Norton who was wounded, not Colonel Neff.)* Both were taken to Beverly Tompkins' house (Sunny Side) where they were both exchanged later. Colonel Gilbert Morgan captured Colonel Neff and got his navy revolver. He allowed me to shoot it, and I read where it was engraved "For Leut. Neff from his friends on Pearl Street, Cincinnati."

The Rebels (as they now call us) pulled up stakes and left Camp Tompkins three days after the battle. Of course, we thought after we had repulsed the enemy there would not be much more trouble and were quite jubilant and expected the Rebels to remain in control of the valley. But wiser ones shook their heads, the end was not yet. We soon heard our men were slowly retreating up the valley. About the 22nd of July, they began passing Paint Creek. The road was full of all kinds of wagons and buggies loaded with women and children and household goods, while cows, horses, sheep and dogs were being driven along with them.

My Uncle Felix Hansford's house was filled to overflowing all day, they must have fed hundreds of citizens. Captain Jenkins' family was among them. Toward evening, the Captain rode in with Cooney Ricketts proudly by his side. In the heat of the afternoon the yard was strewn with soldiers resting. I was well acquainted with a great number of them, nearly all were friends and relatives. My brother Carroll was among them, and we had a long talk about the situation and he told me that in all probability they would not be back in the Kanawha Valley again until spring. I gave him all the silver money I had as he said the notes I had would not be good in "Dixie."

Nobody who has not seen a retreat of an army (although in no haste at all) can conceive any idea of it. We were all standing out in front of my uncle's house looking down on the turnpike watching them go by. The cavalry and baggage wagons went by with the artillery near the last. I remember seeing five or six fine looking officers riding the finest horses I ever saw. They made a splendid appearance in their dark gray uniforms with brass buttons. They wore hats with plumes which they took off and rode with them in hand until they were completely by our group of waving and weeping women. One I noticed in particular was a very tall handsome man who rode a beautiful large black horse. Inquiring who they were, I was told they were officers of Chapman's Battery from Monroe County. *Victoria failed to add that the handsome officer she saw that day was Lieutenant Thomas Teays and that eight years later he became her husband.)*

After our troops had all passed up the valley, we knew the Yankees would not be far behind. At the invitation of Cousin Martha Jane Smith, a number of us went to her house about five miles up Paint Creek. Her husband, Major J.S.F. Smith, was superintendent of the Coal Oil Works and she lived in the company house. We all went up on the railroad that ran there from the river. There was a carload of women, children and nurses. However, it was a large house with 17 rooms and we got along nicely. In a few days we heard that all the Federal Army under General Cox had passed by. So, after saying good bye to all our hospitable friends, we turned our faces homeward. When I arrived home I found my father and brother Charley and the servants safe and all things as when I left. The Federals at that time had not started disturbing the citizens and everything seemed quiet after all the excitement.

CHAPTER SEVEN

THE GREAT FLOOD IN THE KANAWHA VALLEY

DURING THE FIRST YEAR OF THE WAR, A GREAT FLOOD *swept through the Kanawha Valley. It was the highest water ever known, rising to approximately 16 feet above the valley floor. It covered everything from hill to hill and left the town of Coalsmouth completely under water. The deluge hit in late September, wiping out a much needed wartime harvest. Victoria Hansford was there, and she vividly described the tremendous devastation and turmoil the flood caused.*

During the months of August and September we ladies were all busy putting up fruit, jellies, wines, and saving everything we could. We thought the Rebs would be back here to winter as some of them had promised their sweethearts and wives, but we looked in vain.

September was drawing to a close when, on the 25th, it commenced raining. It rained three days and nights, and on September 28, 1861, came the flood. I was aroused about three o'clock by people in boats calling to each other. I got up and went to my upstairs window. Looking out toward the river I saw what I supposed to be a thick fog near the ground. However, after listening and peering through the darkness, I realized it was water.

I went downstairs and woke my father telling him I believed the water was over the road. He said that was foolish and told me to go back to bed. I sat there a few minutes and then concluded to put on my shoes and a shawl and go look for myself. Lo and behold, I found it some 10 or 15 feet up in our yard, the road completely submerged long ago. I made haste back to the house and woke father again telling him it was inside the yard. He could scarcely believe it. He said it was unheard of, no one ever heard of Coal River being completely out of its banks.

Father made haste to get into his pants and boots and took his cane and went to see for himself. He was amazed, he stuck his cane at the edge of the water and said he was sure it would come no higher. However, the next time he checked, his cane was beyond reach.

The water came up, up, up, and the first rays of daylight revealed a fearful sight. The morning was cloudy, cold and foggy and there was so much water you couldn't go anywhere without a boat. Uncle Alva came up in a skiff from his house just below the mouth of Coal and picked me up. We went up the main street opposite Mr. Wheeler's storehouse. All the families on the street were moving out and the water was already in some of their houses.

The river was already filled with all manner of stuff, farm produce, hay stacks, wheat and corn fodder, boats, houses, barns, chicken coops, and corn cribs. Such a sight I never saw before.

The water rose steadily all day and I began making plans for moving out but this was impossible without a boat, as we were completely surrounded by water. I told Jane, our cook, to get supper before the water got in the kitchen which was lower than the rest of the house. The water from Tackett's Creek was coming in at the back of the house and she had to put on her husband's boots to finish cooking, and we all ate in a hurry before the water got in the dining room. Brother Charley decided to go out in the first passing boat and go to Cousin Frazier Hansford's on the hill. Father tried to get me to go with him, but I told him I would not go unless he did. He said the Yanks had not been able to run him out of the house and he was not going to let the water do it. So the colored folks and I stayed with him. We carried the bedding and other furnishings that might be ruined upstairs. They stayed in one room and I in the other. Father, however, stayed downstairs and I sat up with him until about 10 o'clock in front of the fire. It was about then that the water began to creek in around the hearthstone. When the water began to stream across the floor, Father went to bed and I went upstairs to mine. There was little sleeping that night as our two faithful dogs that we had to bring in the house began to prowl and howl, making the night hideous.

Imagine our feelings when we knew the water was from mountain to mountain with the Kanawha, Coal, and

Tackett's Creek all under one great sheet of water. There was no boat in case of entire inundation and no one to call on for help. There was one high point back of the house where our horses and cows retreated. They were able to keep their heads above water and were saved, but they kept up a dreadful noise all night.

During the night several times I called down to Father, "How are you getting along?" He answered, "I am still dry." But the gurgling water was frightening. So the night wore on and finally at daylight we heard the welcome sound of boats coming to our assistance. Father waded out carrying his socks and boots to put on in the boat. They called from the foot of the stairs for me to come down and one of the men would carry me to the boat. However, I would not allow any of them to carry me and asked if they would make some other arrangements. Old Uncle Jake Douglas was one of those kind friends and he arranged chairs in a row to the front door. This allowed me to walk out dry shod.

The water was very cold and we were chilled but they took us clear across to Cousin James Teays' where we got a hot breakfast. Their house was filled to overflowing but Cousin Mary Ann Teays was all cheerful and happy. She said she was glad to be able to return some of the kindness they had received the July before. It was then that people had been kind to them when they had been forced to refugee before the advancing Yankee Army and the Battle of Scary.

A party of us young people that were there got in a boat when the water finally got calm and we went down to Aunt Thenie Wilson's. Here I got out of the boat onto the roof of the porch and went through an upper window. They were all upstairs, black and white, cooking and eating. It had been even worse with them than it was with us. They lived exactly at the mouth of the Coal River and the current was still very strong. Driftwood and logs were floating through their downstairs windows. Oh, it was a fearful sight! Imagine the water extending from Rust Mountain clear across the valley to Teays Hill Graveyard, and we were right in the middle of it. While we were there, a large Yankee steamer came down, running close to the house, adding extra damage with its waves, as several outhouses broke loose and floated away.

By the time I got back to our house the servants had washed it out as the water had receded. They had built large fires in each room and soon it was mostly dried out as it had only been under water about 16 hours. We had a good hot supper and made ourselves very comfortable, considering all things.

After the flood we lost all hopes of seeing the Rebs before winter. There wasn't enough left to keep us, let alone feed an army, as they would have depended on what we could supply them. So the winter came on and 1861 was gone without anything else exciting occurring even with Federal troops all around.

CHAPTER EIGHT

IT BECOMES EVERYBODY'S WAR IN MOLLIE'S NEIGHBORHOOD

THE EARLY PART OF THE WAR SEEMED LIKE A BAD DREAM AS I had to go through so much. Dr. Walls was away most of the time and was rarely home in the daytime. He was the only doctor of note for miles around, most having gone to the army as surgeons. His son, William, first went as a surgeon in an Alabama regiment in '61. In the last three years of the war, however, he belonged to the Stonewall Brigade with Jackson, and as a Surgeon-Major he stood high in the estimation of all.

Jackson was mostly in the Shenandoah Valley from '61 until he died near Chancellorsville where he was wounded. The Yanks were generally retreating in front of them and we would then get to see my stepson William more often. He came home once when Jackson was in Winchester and spent several days with us. I do not remember him getting but one furlough during the entire war. He never was

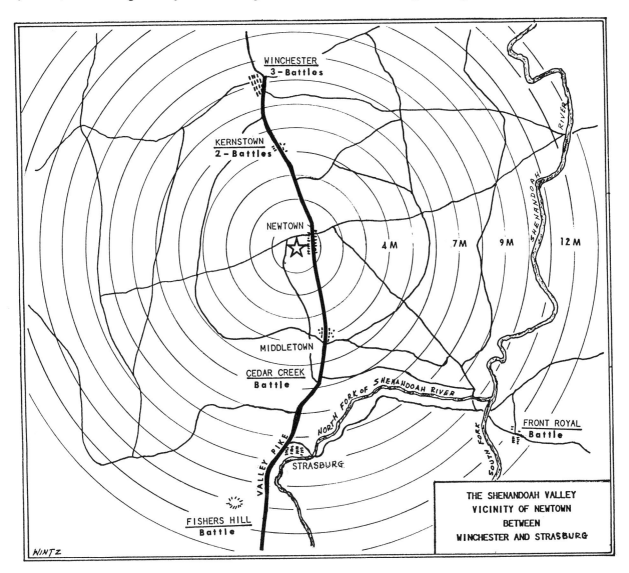

THE SHENANDOAH VALLEY
VICINITY OF NEWTOWN
BETWEEN
WINCHESTER AND STRASBURG

wounded although a ball went through his whiskers and one went through his hat.

William had always been very delicate as a boy and his father dreaded him going in the army, he said it would either kill or cure him. His mother had died with consumption and we always dreaded that. However, he was not in the army a year until he fattened up, spread out and got a better color. When the war ended he was as healthy as anyone.

He was one of the best surgeons and helped take off General Jackson's arm when he was wounded by his own men. Dr. Hunter McGuire did the cutting, Dr. William tied off the arteries and Dr. Coleman administered the chloroform. William has told me many times how Dr. McGuire wanted him to do the cutting but he said, "No, you outrank me and Jackson is too great a man."

Jackson did not die of his wound as many thought, but of pneumonia after his wound was almost healed. When he died his men lost heart and courage; we never had any great victories after that. His men worshipped him and he was a devoted Christian and he never went into battle without a prayer. He said he would do his best and then the Lord would direct all things as he saw fit, whichever way it went.

Dr. William Walls 1837-1886.

House near Guinea's Station, Virginia, where Jackson died of pneumonia following the amputation of his arm.

My sister Cynthia was with me the first two years of the war. She had come from our old home at Coalsmouth to help when my baby boy Hansford was born. She also brought my boy Henry Whiting with her who had begged so hard to come with me when I was married. His mother Jane was given to me by my grandmother soon after my mother died. I was about one year old and she was seven and was to keep me company and help with my care. Jane had six boys and one girl and although they all belonged to me I left them all with my father except Henry. He was a good boy, about 14 when the war started.

Cint used to sass the Yanks and defy them in so many ways that we began to fear for her safety. After considerable arranging by father they finally managed to get her through the lines and safely back home in Coalsmouth.

Mollie's father, John Hansford, wrote the following letters to her brother, Carroll Hansford, and cousin, Frazier Hansford, hoping they could assist in providing a safe way home for Cynthia. The Hansford cousins were both members of the 22nd Virginia Infantry which, at the time, was under General William W. Loring at Pearisburg preparing to launch an attack on the Kanawha Valley. John Hansford's letter was dated August 23, 1862, and 22 days later his son rode into Coalsmouth with the victorious 22nd, having driven all Federal troops out of the valley. Probably whatever plans were made toward getting Cynthia home were discussed at that time.

Coalsmouth, Aug. 23/62
Mr. Carroll Hansford or J. Frazier Hansford.

Enclosed I send $40 which I wish you to remit to Cynthia Hansford by the first safe opportunity, to enable her to come home. You can tell better how to direct her than I can. You will know whether to come to Lewisburg, Va., Staunton or by Richmond to Newburg. If she could get with the Frazier family she could perhaps get through to Charleston before cold weather by some private conveyance.

We are all well, Vic and myself comprise the family. Charles has been at Cannelton since the first of April teaching school. I understand all are well at Clifton.

I direct this to you or Frazier as perhaps she may be situated so as to enable him to attend to it more readily than you can. If it was so that one of you could go and bring her up, I would be glad. She could remain with any of the families until she could come on home.

I could perhaps send her more money to pay expenses. Victoria has written and has doubtlessly given you all local news of the place that would interest you.

Give my respects to all my friends.

Respectfully,
John H. Hansford

There were several women killed in the neighborhood that I knew of. A young girl who lived out in the country had a sweetheart in the Southern Army. One day she saw some cavalry coming toward the house and she went to the door as they were dressed in gray and she thought they were Rebs. The Yanks had many spies and no-counts that dressed in gray and were called "Jesse Scouts." They tried to fool the Southern Army and they did sometimes. When they came near she saw who they were and as she tried to shut the door they all shot through it. She was shot through the breast and bowels but she lived long enough to tell what had happened. Nothing was ever done about it.

I have known them to stop ladies in carriages and take their horses, leaving them to wade home through the mud. No one ever dared to use a good horse as it would surely be taken from them. A Yank started to take my horse once but I persuaded him to go with me and let me ride it home first. We had not gone far before someone called out that Mosby was coming. When he turned to grab my bridle I gave the horse a cut and away I went. He then turned and galloped off with the others. The horse I was on had been with William in the army and seemed to know Yanks when they came near. He would snort, paw the ground and shake his head. Knowing that we would not be able to keep him long, we sent him back to William. Sure enough, in a few days they came back to look for him.

One time I knew of them to stop a hearse and take the horses. It was taking one of our soldiers who had died at home to the cemetery. The old men and boys had to carry the coffin a half mile to the graveyard and then pull the hearse back. Thank goodness, however, they got paid back that time. They had not gone more than a mile when Gilmore's men surprised them and took them all prisoners.

Harry Gilmore, born in Baltimore County, Maryland, January 24, 1838, died in Baltimore, March 4, 1883. Enlisted in the Confederate Army under Colonel Turner Ashby. He was appointed Sergeant-Major for gallantry in action at Harpers Ferry in December 1861. He was severely wounded February 1862. On recovery he was made a company commander and was captured as a spy September 1862. He was exchanged in February 1863 and in May was commissioned Major commanding the 1st Maryland Confederate Regiment. In February 1864 he led General Jubal Early's advance into Maryland. He was severely wounded at Bunker Hill and was captured at Woodstock. He spent three years in Europe and in 1874 was elected Police Commissioner of Baltimore. He published "Four Years in the Saddle" in New York in 1866. — Appletons' Cyclopedia of American Biography, N.Y. 1888

They came marching them back through town on foot on one of the hottest days I ever remember. The Yank who had been in command and had stopped the hearse and had taken the horses was a big fat German. He came along puffing and swearing and tried to sit down in front of our house. Although he had been so mean I felt sorry for him when his guards made him take off his cavalry boots, "so he could walk better." He seemed to be a great coward.

In the first years of the war we used to hide our valuables. After a while we found that it did very little good as they would always hunt the house over, both inside and out. Many people hid their things away from the house and then forgot where they put them. There was a great amount of valuable things that were never found and may be unearthed years from now.

One day the Yankees took Dr. Walls down the street to take the oath. I sat quietly on the porch waiting for him to return. When he came back he was guarded by two soldiers and he gave me his watch and money and told me to hide his box of valuable papers. He supposed he was being sent to prison as he would not take the pledge. He was later released, however, and returned home that night. There were a great many other private citizens who were arrested and sent away and they never knew for what reason.

There was a Southern Methodist preacher that lived on the other side of Winchester who came to preach at our church once in a while. A battle was fought near his place and sometime afterwards he went over the field and picked up several bayonets. He had gotten the idea of making in his shop a set of knives from them with wooden handles. The Yankees came and took him prisoner as he had been accused of making knives out of Yankee bayonets and they claimed the handles were made out of Yankee bones. They knew better but they sent him to Point Lookout anyway.

They were just looking for an excuse to make him a prisoner as they thought he was going to enlist in the Southern Army. They took many citizens away just for the same reason.

During most of the war we had our houses searched every few weeks for Rebs and letters. Every once in a while mail was brought in and hid so well that they never could find it. Men out in the country hauled wood into town all the time and sometimes they would put the mail in a hollow log. They would then say to the lady of the house, "Look to your wood carefully." She would then look until she found the mail and then distribute it. Sometimes some of our men would come through at night and bring in contraband mail.

One cold night when snow was on the ground and the moonlight was as bright as day, I was sitting by the window reading. My baby boy was in the cradle by my side and our little black girl Sallie was asleep by the fire. Suddenly there was a sharp rap on the window and I looked out and saw about twenty Yankees with their bayonets shining in the moonlight. One ordered me to open the window which I did inquiring what they wanted. I was told they had come to search our house for Rebs as some had been reported in town. I told them they were wasting their time as we had been searched every few days and besides they could see the only Rebels here were myself and the babe. They consulted a while and then decided I was telling the truth and if I would give them something to eat they would leave.

I had already cooked some things for Sunday dinner so I gave them half of it. As they left, one remarked that I must be a brave woman to stay by myself at night. I had become accustomed to it as I always tried not to provoke them and did not complain.

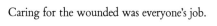
Caring for the wounded was everyone's job.

CHAPTER NINE
GIVING UP THE FAMILY SLAVES

EARLY IN THE WAR THERE WAS A SLAVE TRADER IN TOWN who offered Dr. Walls a thousand dollars in gold for our two house boys, Henry Whiting and George See. He would never sell a Negro, he said absolutely not. I could no more sell them than I could my own children. The man said, "Doctor you will regret this for you will lose both of them and you will need the money before the war is over. Doctor replied, "I need it now but not enough to sell them." Both boys stayed with us until after the war and we had to send them away.

The first year of the war we did not need Shipley, Mary's husband, so Dr. Walls subleased him out in Winchester. He did not belong to us but belonged to a man in Maryland who would not sell him. However, he always hired him out to us so he could be with his wife. Mary was one of the best women I ever knew. She was a splendid cook, washer and nurse as she had been trained well by her former mistress. She had grown children when I first knew her. That was one reason I never brought my own woman Jane from home as I did not need her.

One of Mary's sons, George, went through the war with my stepson, Dr. William Walls, as his servant. When the southern troops drove into Pennsylvania, he was with William at Chambersburg where he could have stayed but did not consider it. After the war, George came back. I was sitting by the fire one morning when someone knocked at the door and I said, "Come in." It was George all dressed up in a fine black suit and a high silk hat. I hardly recognized him until he said, "I's George, Miss Mary, don't you know George, I don come home to stay." I told him I was glad to see him and that he was looking so well but I explained that we could not afford to hire him as we still had Henry Whiting. "But Miss Mary," he said, "I just want to stay. I don learned to cook—you just try me for awhile." So we hired him for about a year and he was a good cook.

However, he had learned so many bad habits in the army that we could not accept so we had to let him go. If he took a notion that he wanted to cook something for dinner that we did not have, he would go out at night and get it. Before we knew where it came from, it was cooked and on the table. When we asked him where it came from he would reply, "Oh, I just went out foraging like we used to do in the army."

In the second year of the war, Banks was in the valley carrying off all the Negroes he could transport. Shipley showed up one morning with a wagon and an escort of 25 Yankee soldiers and said he had come to get Mary. Henry came running in much excited saying, "Oh, Miss Mary, Uncle Shipley has come for Aunt Mary." I went out and the Yanks were already loading up all their things including beds and clothes. One of the soldiers ordered me to "Give this woman a hundred pounds of flour and fifty pounds of meat until they can find work." I said, "I will not, I have fed and clothed them all through this dreadful war and now you can take care of them." He said he would come in and take it and I told him to go ahead as I expected as much from his kind. Shipley then spoke up and said he did not need it as he could support his wife and children.

I then told him I did not want them to go hungry and I would give them something as they had always been good servants. I told him I only blamed him for coming with an armed force when he could have asked me on his own. We would have let her go as we were having it hard just to support ourselves at the time. After the war Shipley came back to see us, he was as pleasant and as humble as he ever was. Mary had died soon after they went to Baltimore, they had such a hard time.

During Bank's retreat when Jackson ran him out of the valley, he still insisted on picking up all the Negroes along the way. When the first wagons began passing by, most of them were filled with Negro women and children. A number of sick and wounded Yanks were walking, having been forced to give up their places in the wagons. Hundreds of black men and boys were also walking while some of the mounted soldiers had Negro women behind them on their horses. The Yanks were furious at having to stop and pick them up during the retreat, but they said that was General Bank's orders.

Most of our servants went to Baltimore where hundreds died of exposure during the first winter. They had been used to wearing thick linsey dresses, yarn stockings and heavy shoes. When they began wearing calico dresses, cotton stockings and thin shoes in all kinds of winter weather, many of them got sick.

Our nurse Cornelia Fletcher had gone to Washington with Doctor's young daughter Mary early in the war. When she was able she sent for the remainder of her family who lived in Newtown. One of her sisters married Lincoln's carriage driver. She was in bad health and when the President was shot she became so upset that she died. One of her other sisters had developed consumption and died soon after. Their mother later came back to Newtown and said she never wanted to leave again.

It was perfectly surprising how well the Negroes did all during the war, even after Lincoln's proclamation. We lived so near the border they could have done a great deal of mischief if they had a notion. They seemed happy since they were not compelled to work. They were fed by the army and they drew rations just as the soldiers but only when the Yankees had control of the area. Some, however, were too proud to take anything. Hundreds of others never left their homes until their "white folks" had to send them off when they became too poor to keep them.

I never knew of but one Negro to spy on the "white folks" and report to the Yankees. He afterwards killed himself by jumping into a well in his master's front yard.

After the war Henry Whiting wanted to stay on with us and was agreeable with what we were able to pay him. Henry had belonged to me and I had brought him from Coalsmouth after I was married. His father had written several times for him to come to Gallipolis, Ohio, where their family had settled. Henry would not go but finally we became so poor that we could no longer pay him and we had to send him away.

The morning he left he could not keep from crying and neither could we. He hugged the horse's neck, petted the dog and gave Hansford his pet rooster. We all went to the depot with him and Dr. Walls bought his ticket. My two children cried and clung to him until he had to leave.

Union Soldiers enforcing the Emancipation Proclamation.

CHAPTER TEN
MOSBY AND HUNTER'S
PRIVATE WAR IN THE VALLEY

I WAS ALONE ONE EVENING SITTING IN MY FRONT ROOM reading when all at once a big Yank broke through my front door. He commenced hunting about, ignoring my presence altogether. He got into the hall closet where he found a bushel of apples which I had just brought in from the country. He walked out the door and down the road with the basket on his shoulder. As the army was passing through, other men saw him come out of my house with the apples and a great many rushed for my door to get some for themselves. They ended up cleaning out everything in the house to eat before they left.

After the main body of troops had passed, only a few stragglers were still moving by. One of them tried to get in and finding the door locked he became furious. He tried to kick the door down, cursing and swearing in the most awful manner. Just about then some of his companions ran by warning him that Mosby was below town and that he better run for cover.

They all feared Mosby as his men would often slash through their wagon trains when they were moving down the Pike. They would usually take 50 or so prisoners and horses, cut out several wagon loads of provisions and be gone before they could stop them.

When the Yankee Army was at Strasburg, they were passing up and down the road often. I remember one cold rainy evening three cavalrymen stopped at our door and

Mosby partisans. VSA

Mosby's men stop at Mollie's house.

got off and came in. They had large gum blankets draped around them so entirely that I could not tell what uniform they wore. I had a bright fire going and they stood in front of it drying out and talking. Not knowing who they were I did not try to say anything to them. Finally, when they started out the door, one raised his gum blanket and said "We wear the gray." They then mounted up and rode off toward Winchester.

It was getting dark and I was home alone with Hansford who was sick with diphtheria. Dr. Walls finally got home and we had to sit up with him that night. About 12 o'clock a soldier came for Dr. Walls to go over to Dr. Miller's to tend to a Yankee who they thought was dying. There had been a skirmish and a wagon train had been attacked by Mosby and the man was mortally wounded. Doctor did not want to go and leave us but thought he better since they had sent for him.

When he came back he said the wounded man had been able to talk and told them what had happened. He said he was riding leisurely along in front of the wagons when three soldiers covered with gum blankets rode up and spoke very polite asking him what regiment he belonged to. They then said they believed they would ride along with him. He said he thought nothing of it as he had one hundred men as an escort. He did not know that they

had fallen back to check on a disturbance at the rear.

All at once one of the men leveled a pistol at him and another took hold of his bridle, but he bolted free with them firing at him in the dark. A soldier who was with the wounded man told them what had happened after that. He said Mosby's men stampeded the wagons and as they passed a side road, more of his men came out and cut about five or six wagons off the main road. He said he heard that they then took off across country to Front Royal.

So the three men who called at my house that evening were Mosby's men waiting to attack the train. A Yankee officer said to me once "Why don't you people get up a petition to withdraw Mosby from the Valley and send it to Jeff Davis. Then you all would not be treated so badly by the Yanks." I told him never, we would rather suffer.

Another time three of Mosby's men rode into town and stopped at Mary Wilson's house to get something to eat. She was a poor widow who sometimes entertained soldiers of both armies. After they had eaten they were riding leisurely up the road in the dark when they rode into the advanced guard of a wagon train. They fired their pistols and leaped their horses over a stone wall and disappeared into the countryside.

This stopped the whole train with a hundred German guards. It was a bright moonlight night and I was standing in my door and saw all the commotion. One wagon driver rolled off his horse and crept in our yard and laid down behind a bush. Other drivers unhitched their teams and rode off leaving their wagons sitting in the middle of the road. It was a scene of general confusion. Officers were shouting orders that no one was heeding, scared horses were squealing and neighing, and an occasional shot in the dark added to the bedlam up and down the road. After things calmed down and the road was cleared, they passed on by and headed toward Strasburg. Since several of the teams had run off in the dark, a number of wagons had been left in a line along the road. Sometime during the night someone had tried to move one of the wagons but only got it as far as the Methodist parsonage where they left it in front of the house.

We heard that when they got to Strasburg and reported to General Hunter they told him they had been fired on by we citizens. The next morning he sent a detail of soldiers back to Newtown with orders to punish everyone who might have had anything to do with the attack.

That morning my boy Henry came running in and told me to look down the street at the Methodist parsonage. It was surrounded by Yankees and he said they were going to burn it down. At that I ran right down there as it was only the third house from ours. When I went in, there was a Yank with an oil can pouring oil all over the furniture. I told him, "You go about this like you are accustomed to burning." He answered, "I am; I have probably burned about 50." At that he began cursing Rebel matches as he commenced to trying to strike them. In the meantime, I caught up the four corners of a table cover that held a picture of Mr. Wolfe's wife, bric-a-brack and several books and ran out with it. Another Yank tried to stop me, said it was General Hunter's orders that nothing should be saved out of the house. By the time I got back to the door, the blaze stopped me and I could get nothing more out.

In the meantime, Mr. Wolfe, who had been preaching in the country, arrived home. When he saw what was happening he ran up the back stairs to try to save his books and papers. Another Yank saw him go up and poured oil on the stairs and set them afire. Mr. Wolfe came running back down dragging his trunk and got his whiskers and hair burned off. He then barely had time to save his horse as they had also set fire to his stable and carriage house. He had lost his wife the year before and his two children were in school. When they came home later and saw what had happened they began screaming and crying. Two neighboring houses also caught fire but we were able to get them out. A young girl who lived in one of the houses begg-

ed them to help her get her piano out. Two soldiers went in and began to help when the Captain came up and ordered them to let it alone. We then tried to get it through the door but it fell and broke off two legs, ruining it.

Reverend John Wesley Wolfe was born in Martinsburg, West Virginia, in 1824 and was converted early in life and joined the church. At the age of 21, he was licensed to preach and in 1846 was admitted to the Conference. He was twice married. In 1850 he was married to Miss Caroline Goodwin, of Botetourt County, and to Miss Eva Mannel, of Clarke County, in 1864. He died in 1894 in Springfield, West Virginia. During his pastorate here the parsonage was burned, by which he lost all that he possessed—including a valuable library—except the clothing he and his family were wearing. General Hunter's chief of staff wrote him a letter of apology, saying it was done through mistake.

REV. JOHN WESLEY WOLFE.

They burned one other brick house in town belonging to Dolph White. The poor widow where Mosby's men got their supper was also punished in a cruel way. When the Yanks went to Mrs. Wilson's they found out that the house did not belong to her. They began carrying out everything in the house and piling it up in the middle of the street. When they got there, her two daughters were away from home and she was out in the yard making soap, wearing her worst clothes. She had a nice trunk packed with her best clothes and they put that on top of the pile. After they had gotten everything out of the house they got a rocking chair and tied her in it. They then poured oil on the pile of furniture, clothing and carpets and set it afire. They did all this because she had given three Rebs their supper and as she said, she also fed Yanks. She sat there and cried and talked to neighbors while her things burned.

After the fire died down and everything was gone, they tied Mary Wilson's hands in front and with a lead rope, a soldier led her off down the road.

They began walking her all the way to Hunter's headquarters which was over five miles from town. About the time they started, it began to rain and although she was sixty years old at the time, she was forced to walk three miles in a downpour. Finally one of the Yanks said "Boys, I can't stand any more of this, what if it was your mother?" With that he got off his horse and put her up in his place and she rode the remaining two miles. She was so tired and worn out by then that she could hardly stand. She thanked the soldier and told him at least she had found one Yankee who had a little bit of feeling for an old woman.

That night they made her take the oath and then let her go, to get back the best way she could. Knowing some people who lived nearby, she made it to their house where she stayed until she was able to travel again.

Additional information concerning General David Hunter's retaliation against Newtown was found in an unpublished paper written by John. M. Steele. He had been a boy in Newtown during the war and had recorded his recollections several years later. The writings belong to his grandniece, Mildred Lee Grove, a well-known local historian living in Stephen City.

John Steele noted that the other brick house that was burned that day belonged to Adolphus "Dolph" White. Dolph White had been the slave dealer that Mollie Walls referred to who wanted to buy their two house boys at the beginning of the war. It was probably because of his past slave business that the Yankees burned his house.

Steele further recorded that a short time after the burning in Newton, some of Mosby's men caught a Yankee soldier in the

neighborhood in the act of burning a barn. He said they brought him into town and took him to Mrs. Nisewander's inn where they got him his dinner. They then took him to the ruins of Dolph White's house, stood him against the brick wall that was still standing and shot him. After painting "Yankee Burner" on the wall, they rode off leaving the townspeople to bury the soldier on the spot.

Sometime after the war, John Steele recalled that Federal agents came around looking for unmarked graves of Yankee soldiers so they could be moved to the National Cemetery in Winchester. He said they were paying five dollars to anyone who could point out such a burial site. He stated that he collected five dollars for showing them the grave of the soldier who was shot at the old Dolph White house.

General Hunter was not born a Yank which made the people hate him that much more. He was a Virginian, a renegade, a traitor to his native state. He acted worse in the Valley than any Yankee ever did. The people liked Sheridan a thousand times better than they did Hunter.

Gen. David Hunter (1802-86), Union general who took over the Department of West Virginia in May 1864. He was repulsed by Gen. Early at Lynchburg in June 1864, and retreated into West Virginia, leaving Washington, D.C. open to attack. He gave up his command on Aug. 8, 1864, and was labeled a "felon to be executed if captured" by President Jefferson Davis for his violent acts in Virginia and West Virginia. WVU

Hunter sent a Colonel of a New York regiment, I have forgotten his name, to make every man in town take the "Iron Clad Oath." If they refused, they were to be taken prisoner and sent off immediately. If they all refused, the entire town was to be burned. They rounded up all the men left in town which were only old men and young boys but they could not get them to take the oath. The Colonel, however, refused to burn the town saying with all the men taken away it would be only the women and children who would be left homeless. Knowing the consequences of his decision, he returned to headquarters and resigned from the army. When he passed through town on his way back north, the ladies waved their handkerchiefs and the old men and boys cheered him.

Mosby then sent Hunter a written notice warning him if he burned the town they would hang all the Yankee prisoners they were holding. That stopped it but they tried to scare us by coming back and ordering everyone out of their houses as they would be returning shortly to burn the town. Many people began carrying things out, some were almost hysterical. I sat calmly on the porch but they never did come back.

According to John Steele's recollections, the officer who refused to burn Newtown was Colonel Timothy Quinn of the 1st New York Cavalry Regiment.

One evening a company of Yankee cavalry came into town stopping at every house looking for something to eat. They were with a battery camped at the upper end of town. Some of them came in our house and said they wanted all the provisions they could get and for me to start cooking and have it ready by the time they got back. They were on the lookout for Mosby's men and said they had to stay all night and help guard the battery. I began baking large flat cakes on the griddle beside the ashes in the oven. When they were done I split them and spread applebutter on them. I had twelve of them finished when Henry called from the front of the house "Oh, Miff Mary, here comes the Yankees like someone's after them." As they went by, we heard several shots as our men came into view close behind. There were only about fifteen Rebs and they went but a short distance above our house when they saw that the entire battery was alerted just up the road so they turned and came back. I waved them down and gave them all the cakes I had baked for the Yanks and they were so pleased. We heard later that the Yanks hurriedly moved their battery out and took off for Winchester claiming they were being chased by a big force of Rebs.

CHAPTER ELEVEN

SPRING OF 1862 COMES TO COALSMOUTH

MOLLIE HAD DESCRIBED HOW, DURING THE EARLY PART OF *the war, she and her family had managed to survive the continual hard fighting in the Shenandoah Valley. In the Kanawha Valley, at the same time, sister Victoria was writing about how the Rebs were managing under Federal occupation.*

As the spring of 1862 came with its warm sun and flowers, it found us with sad hearts and low spirits as some of our boys had died during the winter from exposure and pneumonia. Brothers Charley and Theodore Turner both died a day apart at the residence of Guy French at Prince-

ton, Mercer County, Virginia. They were buried in the same grave away from friends and home but kind hands had administered to their wants and soothed their dying moments. They laid them tenderly and very neatly away, in the Princeton burial grounds. Thorton Thompson also died and was buried far from home. It was indeed a sad thought that these, if not more, would be missing when they came back to our valley.

But we must live on, work on, and hope on, and as before, every seed we planted in our gardens and every flower we raised was for "our boys." We worked with a view to maintain the Rebel Army next winter with full and plenty. We gathered berries to make wine for the sick. We made shirts which we put away for them for by this time things of every kind were getting high and very scarce. So everything we did was for "our Rebels" who were in the Shenandoah Valley of Virginia fighting for us.

One evening in the spring of '62, I was left entirely alone. It was a cold overcast day, and I was sitting by the fire reading some old Dixie letters I had spread out before me. I also had a small silk flag draped over the back of the chair they were on. It was white and red with eleven white stars embroidered on a blue ground. It was what we then called "The Eleven Starred Banner." About then I heard the gate slam and looking out I saw four Yankee soldiers armed to the teeth headed for the door. The orderly sergeant in front wore a sword, a red sash, pistols, etc., etc., etc. Behind him were three men with muskets and I only had time to thrust my letters in the fire. The flag which I so highly prized went into my bosom, all this within a manner of seconds. With my heart pounding and thumping so loud I could hear it, I put on a calm face and met them at the door. They did not knock as they were a low-down squad that had been sent out by the Home Guard to search for contraband articles. The sergeant said he had been told that I had a Rebel Flag which they had come for. I knew I would never give it up so I looked him straight in the eye and said, "If you can find one here you can have it." I also told him he was perfectly welcome to search the house. Finding me so willing for them to search left him standing abashed. I then told him it was not necessary to have brought so many men with muskets, swords, and pistols when there was only one woman in the house to contend with. He finally sat down and I became more polite and entertaining. I told him that I did have some flags he was welcome to. "Where are they?" he said. "There," I said pointing to a framed picture on the wall of all the presidents. There were four small stars and stripes in each corner but he was so ignorant he had a hard time telling them from "Stars and Bars." He finally said if that was all I had I was welcome to keep it. So I bowed them out very dignified, while my little treasure still lay close to my heart.

This taught me a lesson to be always alert and never get caught napping. From then on I kept all contraband articles together so I could dispose of them at a moment's warning. If those four men had been turned loose to search the house I would have lost valuable articles and perhaps been arrested. Our town was under martial law and we were entirely under their power. We learned to be very discrete but we also learned to be very cunning.

The Yankees were always interrogating the Negroes. Most of them were true and steadfast but a few would let out little things that could get us in trouble. However, our colored people never in any way caused the Yanks to bother us, as long as they were with us.

Now and then "Peter Slick" or "Claw Hammer" would stage a raid in our neighborhood against the Yankees. They were two partisan ranger leaders who often made their appearances in the most unexpected places, remaining only an hour or two at any one place.

Some of the ladies would give them a small bag of salt which they could hang on their saddles when they appeared in their neighborhood—they always needed salt. Sometimes we would give them shirts, socks or other clothing when we got the chance. Oh, I remember toward the end of the war when the South became so poor. Our dear soldiers were fighting for us almost ragged and always hungry. We did all we possibly could for them and we all hoped on and they fought on.

I remember one dark, rainy night several girls were staying all night with me. About 10 o'clock we heard a boat quietly rowing up the river. We found out the next morning that James Nounnan and "Peter Slick" (Peter Carpenter), with portions of their companies, had assembled at Mrs. Lasley's and she had given as many as she could a hot supper. They used that boat and several others to cross the river as Wise had burned the bridge after the Battle of Scary. They were on a raid into Yankee lines and daylight found them far away and we did not get to see them.

The night raiders that Victoria wrote about were part of the Confederate resistance forces that operated behind the Union lines during the latter part of the war.

Captain Peter M. Carpenter, alias "Peter Slick," lived in Coalsmouth. He commanded an unattached company of local insurgents who operated mainly between Kanawha and Big Sandy Rivers. In 1864 the company was accepted into CSA service as part of Swan's Battalion Virginia Cavalry.

"Claw Hammer" was the by-name of Colonel Vincent A. Witcher, commander of the 34th Battalion Virginia Cavalry. He had established a reputation as a daring "behind the lines raider."

Major James H. Nounnan was equally successful as a raider with the 16th Virginia Cavalry. He was known locally as having, under a flag of truce, delivered General Jenkins' surrender terms to the Union commander at the Battle of Hurricane Bridge. At Winfield, he also led the raiding party that boarded the steamer Levi during the night and captured Union General E.P. Scammon.

A vivid portrayal of irregulars, partisans or guerrilla fighters for the South in the mountains of West Virginia. WVU

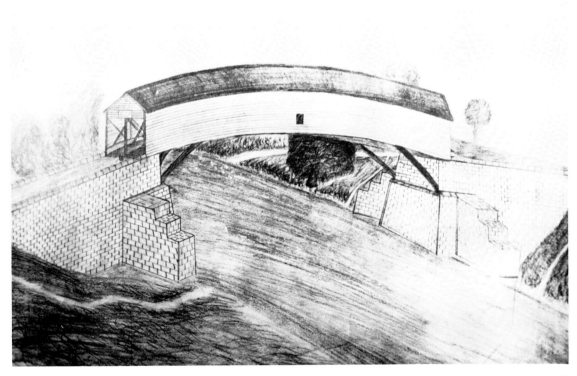

A sketch of the covered bridge over Coal River at present Main Street as it appeared about 1861. The bridge was burned by Confederate troops as they retreated from the Kanawha Valley.

DRAWN BY JOHN N. OVERSHINER, A UNION SOLDIER FROM COALSMOUTH AS HE REMEMBERED IT.

CHAPTER TWELVE

LIGHTBURN'S RETREAT

SO THE SUMMER DAYS OF 1862 WENT BY, FULL OF HOPES AND fears. We had planted our seed and gathered our harvest. The flowers we had planted had bloomed and gone and hearts were growing sad with "hope deferred."

About the first of September, however, our spirits began to rise as rumors told us that we would surely see the Rebels before cold weather. On the 10th of September, the Battle of Fayetteville was fought, and although every precaution was taken to keep us from knowing about the approaching Rebs, we knew almost every move they made. The faces of the Yankees and the Union citizens in town were a thermometer. When they seemed sad and low-spirited it was always a good sign for us. If the troops stationed here were flurrying around sending squads of soldiers out here and there we knew the Rebs were worrying them. All these things now indicated the approach of the Rebels.

On the morning of September 13, my father said to me, "I am sure I hear cannons." When I went out to listen I was sure I also heard cannonading far off. Oh, they were coming, they were coming and I set to work to put my house in order.

About 10 o'clock "Aunt Lucy," an old colored woman, came up from the mouth of Coal and said, "Mrs. Thenie says if you wants to see a sight come down to the Kanawha as everybody from Charleston was on retreat." I got down there in a few minutes, Father and the servants coming along behind. Such a sight I never saw before nor expect to see again. The river as far as the eye could see up and down was covered with boats of all kinds. There were large flat boats, jerry boats, jolly boats, skiffs, and canoes. In the boats were all kinds of people and all kinds of things. My Aunt Thenie Wilson lived on the Kanawha at the mouth of Coal and said it had been going on that way since a little after daylight. When I say the river was covered with boats I mean just what I say. A person could almost cross the river by jumping from one boat to another. They had been looking for the Union retreat and had the boats

ready ahead of time. They were not soldiers but citizens who favored the North and thought it wise to retreat with the Union Army. Several families were on gunwales lashed together. I will never forget one man and woman on one of those rafts. They had all their property in a washtub at one end and she sat at the other end in a rocking chair. The man stood in the middle and paddled and steered the best he could and they both were wet from the water washing over the planks. I felt sorry for them and said to myself, "Poor souls, the Rebels wouldn't have hurt them anyway." But on they went.

Brig. Gen. Joseph Jackson Lightburn (1824-1901)
Commander of the Union troops who were driven out of the Kanawha Valley in September 1862. Born in Pa. but later moved to Lewis County, Va. Organized the 4th Virginia Regt., U.S. Army and was appointed Colonel. Was promoted to Brig. Gen. 1863 and was at Vicksburg, Missionary Ridge, and was wounded during the Atlanta Campaign. He was leading a brigade in the Shenandoah Valley when the war ended. After resigning his commission he was elected to the West Virginia Legislature in 1866. He became a Baptist minister and is buried in the Broad Run Baptist Church Cemetery in Lewis County near Jane Lew, West Virginia. WVA

This was the famous Lightburn's Retreat. Only a small part of the army passed down the road on the other side of the Kanawha. They said the road across the river was jammed with all sorts of people, some walking and others riding. They were in all kinds of vehicles from farm wagons to carts loaded with their belongings. All the time the cannonading continued and it was music to our ears.

Captain John V. Young, Company G, 13th Virginia Volunteer Infantry, commanded the Union troops that occupied Coalsmouth at the time of Lightburn's retreat. He was left in a precarious position as they were separated from the main Union forces that had retreated from Charleston toward Ripley. His only route of escape was down the valley to Pt. Pleasant through an area menaced by roving bands of Rebel home guards and guerrillas. Captain Young's home was just below Coal Mountain in Putnam County, and he wrote the following letter to his two daughters telling them, in part, of his successful withdrawal.

Pt. Pleasant, Oct. 29, 1862
Dear Sallie and Emma:

* * * * *

The military men here think I made a most glorious retreat from Coalsmouth. They think very few men would have conducted the retreat better and I got great praise for it. Some had said that Captain Young would never get out; others said that Captain Young would report at Pt. Pleasant. When Colonel Lightburn came to Pt. Pleasant he inquired at once if Captain Young had gotten out.

* * * * *

Your affectionate Pa
J.V. Young
Capt. Co. G. — 13th Reg. Va. Vol. Inf.

While we were wild with delight, the older people in the crowd looked grave and thought it a dreadful thing and a cruel war. By evening the Rebel cavalry reached Coalsmouth and with them came the sad news of the death of Jimmie Rust. He was the son of Samuel Rust who lived exactly opposite the mouth of Coal. He was killed at the Battle of Fayetteville. He had been in perfect health and perfect spirits thinking perhaps of his home and family which was just a few days off. But alas! God had decreed otherwise. He was brought home in his coffin and buried on a high hill across the Kanawha, first to be laid in the Rust graveyard.

Tombstones of two Civil War soldiers buried in Rust Cemetery overlooking the mouth of the Coal River. James W., son of Samuel E. Rust, volunteered in Co. A, 22nd Virginia Regiment, CSA, 1861, fell in the Battle of Fayetteville, Sept. 10, 1862. Henry Gregory, born April 29, 1839, killed in Confederate Army, April 26, 1863.

Recent view of Coalsmouth taken from the cemetery site on top of Rust Mountain.

Henry Gregory married James Rust's sister, Sarah, and the two young men had grown up together in the vicinity of present-day Walker Street in Nitro. As good friends, on May 22, 1861, they joined the Confederate Army together and served in the same company. After Rust was killed in Fayetteville, his brother-in-law was permitted to accompany his body home with the advancing Confederate forces. On the evening of September 13, 1862, forward elements of the 22nd and 36th Virginia Infantry reached Coalsmouth, only three days after James Rust had been killed.

Less than one year later, Henry Gregory was also killed at the Battle of White Sulphur Springs. Eventually his body was returned home and was buried on Rust Mountain beside his boyhood friend and comrade-in-arms.

William S. Morgan, another young soldier from the area, was also killed at Fayetteville on the same day, September 10, 1862, while serving the 36th Virginia Infantry. However, the Morgan family, from below Scary Creek, chose to let his remains stay buried on the battlefield where he had fallen. Later they marked his grave with an appropriate stone which can still be found there.

The next morning at scarce daylight, my brother came home. I heard a shout from my father and I ran downstairs to find my brother Carroll. He had slept part of the night at Cousin Frazier Hansford's who lived at the Ravenswood farm. Oh, how thankful we were to see him; it was the only time he got home during the war. He was well but rough and sunburned in his butternut suit. He had been gone nearly fifteen months and endured every kind of hardship and privation, just as most others. (There are always some, however, who find soft places anyplace.) Oh, how we loved and petted them, there was nothing too good for them, for we never knew if they would ever come home again. I remember I shook hands with Christopher Crouch that day and he was later killed at the Battle of Dry Creek (White Sulphur Springs).

"Ravenswood" was built by Philip R. Thompson, Jr., and after living in the house for several years, in 1851, he deeded it to Alfred Thornton.

In 1859 James Frazier Hansford acquired the estate, and he and his wife, Annie (Noyes) Hansford, lived there until they died. Family tradition holds that the house was once sold, but since mortgage payments were made with Confederate money, after considerable litigation, the title reverted back to the owner.

During the course of time, a dozen or more owners have made alterations to the house and grounds of "Ravenswood." The most visible change was when the original buff colored brick walls were coated with stucco. It still serves as a residence and is in a remarkable state of preservation.

Greenbottom, on State Route 2 near Lesage, Cabell County, the home of Confederate Gen. Albert Jenkins. It was constructed in 1835 and is still occupied. HPU

Most of Lightburn's army retreated by way of Ripley and then crossed the Ohio River. They had panicked and left a great deal of valuable stores in Charleston which, of course, fell into Rebel hands. Salt was the main thing our army needed and my brother told me he believed that was the main reason they had come back to the valley. He said it would be impossible to winter here as they were too far from supplies of food and equipment. I have heard him say since that after '62 they were never without salt.

General Loring had an army of about six or seven thousand and Lightburn put up no resistance. All the cannonading was done by the Rebs from the top of Cox's Hill overlooking Charleston. The Federals were afraid to retreat down the Kanawha as General Jenkins was waiting for them near the mouth of the river. The few Yankee soldiers who retreated down the other side of the river with the refugees left the valley near Red House and also headed for Ripley. General Jenkins visited his home in Green Bottom during that time and took his wife and children to Dixie with him.

While our hearts were overflowing with joy for the return of our friends, we sadly missed those who would come no more. There were four in number, Charlie Turner, Theodore Turner, Thornton Thompson and Jimmie Rust. I climbed to the top of Rust Hill to see him buried, it was a sad, sad time. I remember my father sympathized with them so deeply. I can see now that he felt for them more than we young folks did. Life was so bright for us that even death could not cast a shadow for long.

We gave ourselves up to the enjoyment of the present, entertaining our soldier boys at our homes, walking, riding, and making them clothes so that they might be warm in the winter. We all knew that they could not winter in the valley. There was not enough to feed them and besides there was danger that the Yankees would return and surround them cutting them off from the main army.

One day late in the fall, a young Rebel by the name of Haymaker came to our house and asked if he could stay all night as he was sick. I prepared a bed close to the fire in Charley's room and said I hoped that would do. He said that was fine for a soldier far from home. He laid down and rested and I went down the street and found everyone greatly excited. The Rebel Army was preparing to move out, going back to the mountains for the winter. When I went back to the house the young man was leaving. When he had heard the news, he staggered to his feet and shouldered his gun. Just turning his face homeward had given him new strength.

And so they must go, all was excitement as everyone was moving out. We had to tell our friends farewell, for how long we could not tell. It might be forever, but we were prepared for anything as everyone seemed to know the time had come for falling back. Some might call it a retreat from the advancing foe but such was not the case. They all left in good order and by nightfall not a Rebel could be seen, nor a soldier of any kind.

CHAPTER THIRTEEN
LIVING UNDER MARTIAL LAW

WE WERE NOW BETWEEN THE LINES. I WILL NEVER FORGET that night. The rear guard of the Confederate lines was along the upper side of Coal River with Yankee scouts on the lower side. Not for one minute did I close my eyes in sleep. All night long the hooting of three owls kept me company. These were Confederate rear guards at the outposts. Their pickets were stationed, one near the mouth of Ramshorn Branch which was directly across the river from my window. Another one was at the mouth of the Coal River. The other lookout must have been near the site where the bridge had been burned. Every few minutes hoo, hoo, hoo sounded dolefully in my ears, one answering the other and so on. It was kept up until the dawn of a gray September morning. Few could have distinguished it from the hooting of real owls but when it ceased I knew our boys were gone. It was now time for us "to take on the burden of life again."

Oh, it was a long, long winter that followed. After the Rebels had gone up into the vasteness of the mountains, the blue coats soon returned and took possession of the valley again. They came back with scowls on their faces. They were incensed at the good treatment we had given our own dear boys. Those who had been kind to them and entertained them were now called to account for it. At least they were made to feel so by bad treatment and harassment.

The officers were a great deal more strict and, of course, we were all under martial law. The soldiers encroached on us in many ways. If it was known that any Rebel had more than he needed to keep body and soul together they came boldly and took it with guns in hand. They took all our corn, the best of our meal, 18 large hams, middlings, all our coal, chickens, turkeys, pigs, and everything else they could get hold of. We dared not open our mouths to the commanding officers or our men could be arrested and sent off to prison and the ladies would be insulted. Our petitions were generally ignored.

Now, of course, there were exceptions as once in a

while we would find a gentleman among them. While following orders as a Federal officer or soldier, it has been known for a few to redress our wrongs when proven and return our stolen property. I will here relate such an incident in which I was a part.

It was in June 1863 when Uncle Alva Hansford came up from his house at the mouth of Coal one morning. He said Sam Rust who lived across the Kanawha had been trying to call over and tell him something but he couldn't figure it out. He had understood him to say, "Tell the Major (meaning my father) there are three white feet and one black one over here in my pasture. If he could think of any plan to get him back on his side he should do so." According to Yankee orders no one was to cross the river without a pass. However, when there was no one near, Uncle Alva rowed over close enough to talk (he dared not touch the bank). Mr. Rust told him our horse was in a herd the Yankees had pastured in his field, which they had brought down from Charleston. It had been over a year since they had taken him from us. Father thought it was not worthwhile to try to get him back but since he had been my riding horse, I determined to try. (See Appendix E—Biography of Alva Hansford)

I went to Charleston and asked the commanding officer to return my horse. He treated me nicely and much to my surprise he gave me an order for me to get him back. When I went to Mr. Rust's, however, to pick him up, I found they had just moved the herd back to Charleston. Sadly disappointed, I was crossing back over the river when a large steamer was passing upstream. Since I had money with me I hailed her and went back to Charleston. I found the same officer and laid my complaint before him and he seemed dismayed that his orders had been slighted. He told me where the herd was in Charleston and said if I could find him the order would still release him to me. I got an old gentleman I knew, Dr. Caldwell, to go out to the government stables with me and there we found "Old Boston."

When I presented my order to an old hostler he cursed and swore and said he was not my horse as he had owned him for years and that I could not have him. Back I went to the officer and this time he went back to the stables with me. As we went along I described the horse to him. I told him he had three white feet, one black, and a mark under his mane. When we arrived at the stables they had changed my horse for a very fine spirited horse. They had put him in the same stall thinking I would claim the better horse and then they could prove to the contrary. I boldly stated that this was a finer horse but it was not mine. The officer then turned to the old wagoner who had cursed and grumbled before and ordered him to "Bring the lady her horse." Whereupon he finally brought him forth. The officer put the rope bridle in my hand and I walked away triumphantly.

I then went to my cousin's, Mrs. Roxy Smith, wife of Colonel Ben Smith, and stayed all night. They took care of my horse and the next morning she loaned me a saddle, bridle and riding habit. I mounted old Boston and rode him to Coalsmouth. The nearer we got to our house the livelier he became as he seemed to remember the old trails we had traveled together. I finally dropped the reins across his neck allowing him to take his own way home. When he reached the front gate he threw his head high and neighed when he saw my father sitting on the porch reading. Father was indeed glad to see me return with our only horse.

During the winter we wrote and heard from our soldier boys quite often by the underground railroad. Once we got word that mail was coming in and we had to figure how to get outside the lines to pick it up. I talked the girls into trying and I was to lead the way through the picket lines. They were Thenie Wilson, Mat Wilson, Lou Lasley, Allie Lasley, and myself. Our plan was to try to pass the guards as if we had not the slightest idea of being halted and if we were, to try and talk our way through.

As we approached the guard post, the sentinel halted us and I told him we were going down the road to see a sick girl and take her something to eat.

'Well," said the sentinel, "I would not even let my own mother pass through here to see anybody."

"Not just to go to that house you can see from here?"
"No."
"Where is your sergeant?"
"In the tent."
"Tell him to come out."

When he came out he was a weak looking man so I began to tell him how we must go see Lena Crouch, the sick girl. We also told him if he would let us pass we would send him a pie for supper. I saw him begin to weaken and went on piling up excuses why we should pass. We also kept piling up promises of the good things to eat we would bring him. At last, after considerable discussion, he gave in and let us go. We did not stay long, however, because the mail was not there. After we visited the sick girl we returned to Thenie Wilson's house and lo, we found the bundle of letters had been left there while we were gone. To this day none of us know how it got there nor did we care as we were just happy it had come. The sergeant's pie and good things were forgotten. However, the next day we inquired about sending the guards their dinner and were told they were all in the guard house. Seemed like they had let some girls go through the lines the day before. The way to a man's heart is through his stomach is the moral of this story.

Letters received from the "Underground Railroad," as we called it, were sent through friends who were able to run the blockade. Sometimes we would get a letter mailed inside the Federal lines from the very heart of Dixie. Often a whole package of letters came and we did not know how or by whom they were delivered. We asked no questions as we knew it was quite important that our right hand not know what the left hand was doing. Sometimes we were notified by a friend that letters were left at a certain place would be sent to friends in Dixie. We left our letters as directed and they generally went through.

The letters we received were often directed in a strange way so that if they fell into Yankees' hands they would not get us in trouble. For instance, I had in my possession a large bundle of letters to distribute. One of them puzzled me a great deal. It was addressed "To Callie," that was all. As the letter was unsealed I thought it best to read it for some other information. It commenced "Dear Wife" and was signed "I" only. After some thought I came to the conclusion it was directed to Mrs. Callie Quarrier Smith who lived in Charleston and was the wife of Major Isaac N. Smith. It had come around through the back counties and had been on the way some time. I doubted very much if it had not gone through my hands she would have received it.

CHAPTER FOURTEEN
MOLLIE DESCRIBES BANKS' RETREAT

I SHALL NEVER FORGET GENERAL N.P. BANKS' RETREAT. It was both a tragedy and a comedy combined. About daylight we heard cavalry passing but since that was a common thing we thought nothing of it. We had not heard from Jackson or any of our boys for several weeks as Banks was between us and Strasburg.

The morning was bright and beautiful and on stepping out on my porch before breakfast, I saw several Yanks running through a garden across the road. They crossed the fence and as one was wounded they stopped to help him out to the roadside. I called to them and asked what was going on. One called back that Jackson was right behind them as Banks had been cut off at Front Royal. Before he hurried off he called back warning me to get inside as skirmishing was going on all around.

Not long after, we could hear a great rumbling of wagons coming when they were still several miles away. When they finally came into view they were all under whip and lash. Most of the first wagons were filled with Negroes as it was Banks' orders to pick them up all along the road.

Next came the supply wagons which were being hard pressed and I never saw such confusion in all my life. Some of the wagoneers cut their horses loose and rode off on them leaving their wagons in the road. Abandoned wagons were set afire and for miles you could see them burning and they were all full of provisions. There was one left in front of our house loaded with groceries. A soldier was about to set it afire when we ladies begged him not to. He refused at first but then at last he agreed not to if we promised not to leave any of the things for Jackson's men. It was loaded with items we could not buy at any price such as sugar, coffee, rice and tea. We ladies quickly carried the things into our houses by the buckets full as we knew that someone else would soon come along and set fire to the wagon.

Another wagon loaded with pickled pork was left nearby but the Yanks knocked the heads out of the barrels and dumped the meat in the road so the Rebel cavalry would have to ride through it. They continued to go by pell-mell all day throwing things away as they went to lighten their loads. One man threw a sack of bacon in my yard and another threw a gum blanket over my fence. Discarded blankets, canteens and haversacks were so numerous they lined both sides of the road.

There were also dozens of horses running loose and I could not stop my black boy Henry from herding them into our back lot. When Dr. Walls came home he made him turn them all out. Henry begged mightily to keep them as they had earlier taken one of our horses and a cow. Several wagon loads of new tents were unloaded in the road until they were piled higher than the second floor windows of the nearby houses. Some Sutler's wagons were also abandoned, filled with all kinds of canned goods. Jackson's men took possession of them and enjoyed them to the fullest.

At that time they called Banks' army, "General Jackson's Commissary." Jackson drove them all the way to the Potomac and what a glorious time we had going along behind. Everyone who had any kind of conveyance followed after Jackson the next morning. What a sight the road was, it was strewn the entire seven miles to Winchester with hundreds of haversacks and canteens. Most remarkable of all was the hundreds, if not thousands, of letters and photos that had been discarded. Why they should throw them away was so strange to me. My black boy Henry was with us and he might have picked up 50 photos. They were little gems, tin types, and even old-fashioned daguerro types. He also picked up hundreds of letters.

In looking through some of the letters when we got home we never found a well-written one in the lot. Most of them were no better than the greenest school child might have written. Others were the most obscene creations that anyone could imagine. I went over hundreds of these letters and most of them commenced with "I take my pen in hand" and with a little (i) or "I hope this will find you well." I have always heard about the great education in the north but these letters did not show it.

CHAPTER FIFTEEN
THE SICK AND THE WOUNDED

IT WAS IN '62 JUST AFTER A BATTLE AT KERNSTOWN AND THE Yanks had control of the area. There were hundreds of wounded from both sides in Winchester. I and a friend, Mrs. John McLeod, decided to go to town and shop and to take some things for our wounded. The Yanks had plenty but our men had to depend on the citizens for extras. We went in our carriage with Henry driving. It was a cold March day but we had no trouble getting into town as the pickets let us pass. We did have to go directly to the Provo office and get a permit and a pass. To get a pass we had to take an oath to the U.S. in which it said, "Give no aid or comfort to the Confederates." If we would not take the oath we could not buy anything or talk to our wounded. I would not take the oath but Mrs. McLeod did so she could do what she wished. They even went so far as to assign a guard to go with me to make sure I did not buy anything or stop to see any of our men.

We went to Mrs. McLeod's brother-in-law's house and since it was cold, the guard agreed to go in with me where it was warm. There was a large stove in the hall where we waited. Mrs. McLeod went down the street and left us there. Soon after she left the guard went to sleep as it was warm and comfortable there.

I slipped out and went to a nearby store and bought what I needed. I remember I got a common balmoral skirt that usually cost 50 cents but I had to pay $7.00 in greenbacks for it. I also had to pay $5.00 for a common pair of boys shoes. When I got back the guard was still sleeping and had never missed me. When we started home we had to pass the home of Dr. Walls' sisters. I asked the guard to let me stop at the door and ask how they were. He agreed and we found them at dinner. Of course, they insisted that we come in and eat something and the guard was perfectly willing. When we started home we left the guard at the picket post and he told them they did not have to search the buggy as he had been with us all the time and we had not bought anything. So off we went toward home rejoicing with about $50.00 worth of merchandise.

Just after the Battle of Antietam in Maryland, when both armies were so crippled, Jackson came back across the Potomac and gradually withdrew up the valley. There were so many wounded that they hadn't near enough conveyances for them. Hundreds came walking up the Valley Pike rather than stay in Winchester where they feared they would fall in the hands of the enemy.

It was very warm weather and there had been no rain for some time and the dust was awful. Many of the poor fellows would give out and lay down beside the road. We had a small empty building near the roadside that Dr. Walls had once used as an office. I got some other ladies to help and we cleaned out the place and furnished it with wash bowls, towels and plenty of old linen. We would stand at the door as the walking wounded passed and bring in the ones we thought we could help. We helped them wash up, dressed their wounds and let them rest a while. Many of them had never even had their wounds looked at and were walking dangerously wounded in the hot sun. Oh, how pleased they were just to find some shade to rest in and get a chance to wash off some of the dust. Some would stay until our little hospital would get so full they would have to move on.

I remember one fine looking tall man was shot through the breast and the ball had come out under his shoulder. He had torn up his shirt and tried to bandage it and without a shirt his back was almost blistered. I undertook to wash and dress his wound but found it in such an awful state that I fainted. I am not easy to faint and probably never fainted a half dozen times in my life. I soon got over it and ran home and got one of Doctor's old shirts for him. When I helped him get it on, he laughed and said it was the first white shirt he had worn since he had been in the army. He thanked me and said he felt much better but that he must go on. However, I feared the Yanks would get him as they were not far behind.

There was one soldier who came in very early one morning. He had been lying out by the roadside all night.

Walking wounded.

He did not seem so badly wounded nor was he suffering. He just wanted to get something to eat and rest. We put him in the little upstairs room where it was quiet and private. When we checked on him that evening, we found he could not speak or eat. I ran and got Dr. Walls at once and he came and found he had lock jaw. He died that night; we knew he belonged to a Louisiana regiment but we never knew his name. He was the only soldier who died in our hospital.

There were several who were sick and worn out, some with chills and a few with malaria fever. They would stay several days, rest up and move on. There was one young fellow from Augusta, Georgia, who asked me to let him stay at our house after we closed the hospital. His last name was Wimberly and he had a Negro boy that had been with him ever since he left home. Not only was he sick but he had a painful arm wound. He was in the ranks and the poor young fellow had never worked a day in his life until he joined the infantry. Oh! he said, I thought it would be so nice to wear a uniform, hear the band music and have all the ladies give you flowers and wave their handkerchiefs. But I soon found out after the first week it was not that way at all. After the first month of marching I thought I

would die and I believe I would have if Tom had not been with me. He did so much for me and all the time he was more homesick than I was. He is a good boy.

Wimberly stayed with us for a month during which time he wrote his father to come after him. He finally came with an ambulance and they left for Richmond intending to get him a furlough to go home for a while. I never heard from him afterwards but he gave me a fine gold pin when he left. He said it was all he had and he wanted to give me something for my kindness.

According to Mrs. C.W. Wimberly of Waynesboro, Georgia, the following information regarding the soldier who stayed with Mollie is supplied.

William T. Wimberly, born about 1838, was the son of Wiley and Lockey McCollum Wimberly. Enlisted in Burke County, Georgia, August 1861 in Company E, Cobb's Legion. Was wounded in Maryland and was discharged near Richmond in 1862.

After the war it was said he had little use of one hand due to wounds. He married Edla C. Powell in Burke County, Georgia, in 1865. Died in Augusta, Georgia, in 1890.

Bringing in the wounded. HFNHP

I tried to forget when they brought the wounded into town. The worse time was after the Battle of Cedar Creek in the fall of '64. I went into a storehouse full of wounded and the poor fellows wrapped in their blankets were lying so close together on the floor that they looked like rolls in a pan. I had a basket filled with baked apples and some other delicacies to give out. One got my attention and I gave him a baked apple. As I looked down at him, I saw a man with large black eyes and a good face, he reminded me of my brother Carroll.

I knelt down and asked him where he was from and he answered Kanawha County. That excited me and I asked him if he was ever in Coalsmouth, my old home. Oh yes, he said that is where I was mustered in the army and where I first joined my regiment. Then I knew he was in the Northern Army so I asked him if he knew any Rebs there. Oh yes, he said most of the best people were Rebs. He then asked me if I knew old Major Hansford who had daughters who were two of the most fierce Rebs he ever knew. He said, "We would always try to get the boat first when we had to set them across the river. They would always run down the Yankees and snub us like we weren't even there. It was fun." I then told him that Major Hansford was my father and the girls were my sisters. He was really surprised and wanted to know what I would be ministering to a Yankee. I told him that he was wounded

and needed help and that I always did what I could for the wounded of either army.

He said he would like to get someone to wash his clothes and I told him I would get my black boy to do it. He insisted on me taking his pocketbook as he was afraid it would be stolen even though he only had $5.00 in it. He also wanted me to write a letter to his mother. He told me his name was Sergeant Griffith and that his mother lived at Barboursville in Cabell County. I told him I had no pencil or paper but that I would come back the next day and write for him.

The next morning was bright and cool and I went down to the storehouse early and found out they had moved most of the wounded to the Lutheran Church. As I got to the church door I saw four dead men wrapped in their blankets lying nearby on the ground. A guard and a regular soldier were standing near them and the soldier was sobbing. I heard him say, "My poor brother, I knew if he was sent to this valley he would never get out alive." I asked him why they had come here to fight us anyway. "Oh, I don't know," he replied. "I wish Lincoln and Jeff Davis were both hung."

Just then a Yankee sergeant came out and I told him I wanted to see Sergeant Griffith. "Why would he want to see a Rebel?" he answered. I told him we were from the same part of the country and I had promised to write a letter to his mother for him. He went inside and when he came back he said I could go in. After looking for some time I found the poor fellow but he was dying. He could not speak but oh, his eyes. I can still see them now. Anyone who could have seen his eyes could never doubt that man has a soul. I told him what I was writing and if it was all right to raise his hand, and he did so. I sat by him until his last breath and then went home crying.

I could not speak of him for a long time without crying. Dr. Walls said that I made such a fuss over that Yank that anyone would think he was a relation. I sent the letter to his mother with the $5.00 but I never heard if she got it. I have often thought of that poor soldier's eyes as he looked at me that bright Sunday morning.

Mollie Walls was able to identify the Union soldier who died that day only as Sergeant Griffith. She also said that he had been at Coalsmouth, Kanawha County, early in the war. By reviewing the rosters of the Federal units stationed at Coalsmouth, **Lewis L. Griffith** *appeared to be the name of the soldier in question.*

His name and organization was forwarded with a request for records to the U.S. Army Military History Institute, Carlisle, Pennsylvania. The following information was received on a copy of a standard military form.

Termination of Service Order

I certify, on honor, that Lewis L. Griffith, a 1st Sergeant of Captain John V. Young's Company G of the 13th Regiment of Infantry Volunteers of the State of West Virginia, born in Kanawha County, State of Virginia, aged 22 years; 6 feet 3-3/4 inches high; light complexion, black eyes, black hair, and by occupation a farmer, having joined the company on its original organization at Coalsmouth, and enrolled in it at the muster into the service at Coalsmouth, on the 23rd day of May 1862 by Captain John V. Young, to serve the regiment for the term of Three Years and having served honestly and faithfully with his company in The U.S. Service to the date of his death, October 20, 1864.

Given in duplicate, at Cedar Creek, Virginia, this 20th day of October 1864.
John V. Young
Captain
Commanding Officer

The morning after Cedar Creek. A scene at a church improvised as a hospital.

There was also a Mother's Claim for Pension Form which was filed the 13th of June 1865, before John Slack, Clerk of the County Court of Kanawha by Sara Griffith, aged 64 years, a resident of the County of Cabell and State of West Virginia and doth on her oath make the following declaration; that she is the widow of Alexander Griffith, deceased, and the mother of Lewis L. Griffith, deceased, who was a Sergeant in Company G, 13th West Virginia, Volunteer Infantry, commanded by Colonel Van H. Bukey in the War of 1861, who died at Newtown in the Shenandoah Valley on the 20th day of October 1864 of wounds received in the Battle of Cedar Creek on the 19th day of the same month.

Witnessed by:
John V. Young
John N. Overshiner

It should be noted that Sergeant Griffith's Certificate of Death and his Mother's Claim for Pension were both signed by his Company Commander, Captain John V. Young. This is the same Captain Young who commanded Company G, of the 13th West Virginia Volunteer Infantry, USA, that occupied Coalsmouth before Lightburn's retreat, September 13, 1862. His home was in Putnam County just below Coal Mountain.

The Mother's Claim for Pension was also signed by John N. Overshiner, who, too, was from Coalsmouth. He was the artist who drew the picture of the covered bridge as it was before the war. (Copy seen elsewhere in this book.)

Another member of the 13th West Virginia Volunteer Infantry, USA, from Coalsmouth was 1st Lieutenant John S. Cunningham. In his letters to his wife, included in Chapter 19, he often referred to the welfare of both Mr. Overshiner and Captain Young.

From Victoria's writings, it could be assumed that all the families in Coalsmouth were pro-Confederate. However, that was not necessarily so. It appeared so only because she chose not to recognize any of her northern neighbors.

Not only did the 13th West Virginia Federal Infantry contain a number of local soldiers, it was commanded for a time by Colonel Rutherford B. Hayes, who would become a President of the United States. The regiment also compiled an impressive record as can be seen from the picture of its battle flag, included in Appendix F.

After one of the battles in the fall of '64, a young lady of our town was out on the common helping with the wounded. She came across an officer with a new uniform that was unusual then as it was of beautiful blue-gray

English cloth. He was lying with his head on a rock and one leg of his pants had been cut off by a Yank surgeon who had looked at the wound. There he had lain for several days with the sun in his face all day and the frosty dew that chilled him through the night. She set about making him as comfortable as possible. She brought him blankets, things to eat and pen and paper to write to his mother in the South. She even mailed the letter for him which was a great undertaking at that time. As soon as he was able to be moved, he was taken north to prison.

A year after the war he wrote the young lady and asked her to meet him in Winchester. They met in front of the Taylor House and she invited him to visit her home and meet her mother. They were married in a few days, and he took her south to live on a large plantation. Her name was Miss Lauck and she later returned and took her mother home with her.

Some of the most happy and exciting days of my life were spent during the war. But there were also many sad and dreadful days. No one except those who have experienced it can imagine what exultation and happiness one feels after a great victory, nor to suffer the deep heart-felt misery of defeat. Oh! to see all those dead and wounded young men lying around by the hundreds. It is like no other sorrow as victory is like no other joy.

Union soldier George Washington Smith, father of Gen. Sheridan Smith—longtime Nitro resident. He was a member of the 13th West Virginia Volunteer Infantry.

CHAPTER SIXTEEN

WE ALL TOOK IN THE WOUNDED

ONE MORNING WE FOUND A WOUNDED REBEL SOLDIER AT our front gate. As the Yankees were in control of the area, I had him brought in the house and put in the small room upstairs. His wound was dangerous but with proper care, we expected him to recover. He tried to be cheerful but he was afraid the Yanks would get him and send him to prison. When we had him brought in I had our young servant George prepare a room for him. We had an old clock in the room that had not been running for years, and while he was fixing the bed, it began striking until it struck twelve. "Oh, Miss Mary, that man is agonna die cause that old clock is striking." I laughed at him but I could not get him to go back up to the room. The next morning while a neighbor lady was sitting with the soldier, three Yanks came in my kitchen and wanted something for breakfast. When they left they each took something, one even took a pan of bread out of the oven.

Just after they left, the lady upstairs called for me to come up right away. When I got there I found the blood was streaming from the young man's wound down on the floor and he was so far gone he could not speak. He had become excited when he heard the Yanks down stairs and had tried to move. He died soon after and we never knew his name. We buried him out back without the Yanks ever knowing he had been there. I could never account for the old clock striking as it never struck afterwards.

There were at least seven of our men left in town that did recover. In most cases the ladies at whose houses they stayed managed to smuggle them through the lines to Dixie as soon as they were well enough to travel. One I remember, a Miss White, nursed one young soldier and when he was able she took him in an old sleigh with a borrowed horse, pretending she was going to the mill. She got him through the lines to a friend's house in Strasburg. From there he was sent on and soon rejoined his regiment. As was often the way, he came back after the war and mar-

The wounded was everyone's job. HFNHP

-54-

Wounded soldier and pretty nurse sparked many wartime romances. VSA

manners seemed to improve and she began to keep herself tidy and neat.

Several years after the war, the soldier returned and married the girl. One evening after the wedding she called to see us and bid us good bye. Dr. Walls did not know them as they had become the finest looking couple you could imagine. He said, "Doctor, I could not think of not coming to see you as you and my wife saved my life. I have come back to take her south with me to my home in Florida." We heard from them often as she used to come to Virginia to spend her summers. After Mrs. Nisewander's husband died, they took her south to spend her last days with them. She afterwards sent Dr. William Walls a parrot that she had taught to say "Good morning Dr. Walls" and other things. I suppose it is still living as it was young then and they live a long time.

ried the young lady and took her south.

It was in '64 that a young Confederate was stricken with typhoid fever and was left at Mrs. Nisewander's hotel in Newtown. Dr. Walls tended him and since he was very low, he feared he would not get the needed care at the hotel. Dr. became interested in him as he seemed such a nice young man, and he spoke of him often. One day he told me that the little girl who lived at the hotel had started nursing him and although she was only 13 years old, she was doing very well. At last, above all expectations, he finally got well and was able to go back with his regiment.

This little girl was very pretty and she had a romantic history. Several years before I came to Newtown, there was a woman who came to the hotel walking through the rain and mud and asked to stay all night. Mrs. Nisewander was a kind-hearted woman and since she had a small babe, she took them in. The next morning she found the mother very sick and in a few days she died, leaving the baby. They never knew who she was or where she came from so Mrs. Nisewander kept the baby. As she became older, she learned to help in the hotel. Although she grew to be wild and rough in her manners, she was soft hearted and could be very gentle at times. After she had nursed the soldier her

Home care was the best care. HFNHP

CHAPTER SEVENTEEN

WHEN SHERIDAN WAS IN THE VALLEY

WHEN SHERIDAN WAS IN THE VALLEY, THERE WAS A SKIRmish through town and several Yanks were wounded and left in the neighborhood. A Yankee colonel came back one morning to see one of his men who was among them. When the lady of the house where the soldier was heard that his name was Capehart, she told him there could be a relation of his in town, referring to me. The colonel rode on up to our house with his orderly and asked to see me. I invited him in and Dr. Walls came home soon after. Colonel Capehart told us who he was and we determined that two of his uncles married two of my mother's sisters, that was the only relationship there was. He said he lived near Wheeling and had been a doctor there before the war. We found him to be an intelligent, nice man and I asked him how he came to be in the Northern Army. He explained and we were satisfied. When he left, Dr. Walls invited him to come for breakfast the next morning and bring his brother Lieutenant Colonel Charles Capehart who was in the same regiment. Their camp was in a "skift" of woods in sight of our house, but they were ordered away at daybreak. He sent his orderly with his regrets and a signed photo of himself.

Evidently Mollie Walls never knew at the time or learned afterwards that both of the Capeharts had established outstanding military records as Union Cavalry leaders. Colonel Henry Capehart commanded the 3rd Cavalry Brigade while Lieutenant Colonel Charles Capehart led the 1st Regiment West Virginia Volunteer Cavalry. Both commands were part of Custer's 3rd Cavalry Division.

The brothers' greatest individual recognition came in the forms of Congressional Medals of Honor. Colonel Henry Capehart received the nation's highest award for heroic action on the Greenbriar River in 1864, and Lieutenant Colonel Charles Capehart was presented the coveted medal for exceptional action at Gettysburg.

Henry Capehart was born in 1825 in Cambria, Pennsylvania, the son of John and Sophia (Stackhouse) Capehart. He attended medical college in Philadelphia, after which he married

Elizabeth Kinsey and began practice at Bridgeport, Ohio, near Wheeling. He was commissioned surgeon of the 1st West Virginia Cavalry, USA, in 1861 but was later appointed Regimental Commander with the rank of Colonel.

After the war, he returned to Bridgeport where he continued his practice. His son, Edward E. Capehart, graduated from the Naval Academy and was a distinguished naval officer during the Spanish American War. Henry Capehart was breveted a Major General USV, June 17, 1865. He died April 15, 1895, and is buried in Arlington Cemetery, Washington, D.C.

Union Col. Henry Capehart was a relative of Mollie Walls. HFC

General Capehart's tombstone in Arlington Cemetery. AC

I met many nice gentlemen in the Yankee Army. There were bad men in both armies, of course. There were also cowards in both armies, but some of the Northern Army were great cowards. The Southern men did not make such a display of cowardice. Everyone knew that the Southern Army was made up of better material than the North. Generally, they were men from the cities and factories. Some Yankees from New York were camped nearby with whole companies of foreigners, mostly Germans, who could not speak a word of English except for their officers. Of course, they could not feel the same interest in fighting as did our men who were protecting their homes and families. No one except those of us who were in their midst could know as we who saw it.

Mollie was probably referring to elements of General Louis Blenker's all-foreign "German Division." Although many of Blenker's men had previous military experience in Europe, they were generally viewed with suspicion and distrust even by their own Federal high command.

In the spring of '62, they were dispatched from their camp near Arlington to reinforce Freemont's Mountain Department somewhere in West Virginia. Their trek turned out to be one of the worst fiascoes of the war. The six-week march became famous, due to neglect by the War Department. The 10,000-man command was sent out without basic military necessities, including maps, medical supplies, tents, and foul weather gear. As a result, the men had to sleep in the open during periods of excessive rain and snow causing extreme discomfort to the entire command. They soon consumed all their provisions with no prearrangement to replenish them while in transit. Consequently, they were reduced to foraging, looting, and thievery.

Lacking accurate maps, they frequently became lost. Although Banks was supposed to see that Blenker's division was guided toward Freemont, he did little more than comment on their wanderings in his reports. Finally, General Rosecrans found

Blenker on the lower Shenandoah and directed him to the vicinity of Winchester. The men were in such bad shape that they never again were able to become an effective fighting unit and were finally broken up into smaller organizations and reassigned to other already seasoned commands.

The experiment of having a Union division made up almost entirely of foreign-born troops had been a failure because of biases, poor generalship, and bad luck. However, there was no lack of devotion and heroism among the foreign-born soldiers.

One evening I was sitting alone when an old Negro woman in the neighborhood named Clara came to the door crying and wringing her hands. She sobbed, "Oh, Miss Mary, I have killed a Yankee." "When and where?" I asked. "Down at my house, I was out in the yard cutting wood when I heard someone in the house. I ran to the door and saw a Yankee inside searching through my drawers and he had thrown all my things on the floor. He had found my money and was counting it with his back toward me. The devil told me to hit him with the axe and I did. I knocked him down and then I ran. I know he was dead as he never moved. Oh, my, my, they will come and kill me and burn my house." I told her the doctor would soon be home and we would go and see what could be done.

After the doctor came, we went to her house but we found the Yank had crawled off. The floor was covered with blood and everything was dumped out of her drawers. She found that her money and several other little keepsakes were gone. We heard the next day that a soldier had been thrown from his horse in town and got his skull cracked. He was probably afraid to say that he had been robbing a poor old Negro woman whom he was supposed to be defending from the cruelty of the Southerners. Dr. and some other men in town started a collection in town for old Clara, everyone gave something.

When Sheridan's Army wintered a mile from our town, everyone could ask for a home guard. I wrote a note to a General Emory for one and he sent me a German who could scarcely speak a word of English. I did not like him so I sent him back. He then sent a young man from Buffalo, N.Y., named John Flint. After he found out we would not betray him to Mosby's men, he would do anything he could for us.

We were at that time behind the Yankee lines and were not allowed to buy anything in the way of goods without an order from the Provost Marshall. To get one, we had to take the oath of allegiance to the U.S., the "Iron Clad Oath," as we called it. We never would take it but when Mr. Flint would hear us say we needed something he

would go to the Sutler's and buy it for us. We would always pay him back although he did not expect it. I found Mr. Flint to be more help than any servant I ever had. He went ahead and did whatever he could without being asked. I always had full hot meals three times a day on Dr. Walls' account. He was riding all the time but he always tried to get home at meal time. He was so pleased with my cooking and management without servants.

Mr. Flint had been raised to work. He came in the army as a substitute for a rich man in New York like thousands of others did, I suppose. That was the reason we scarcely ever met educated, refined Yankees in the ranks. The officers were generally well raised, intelligent, and some were even good natured, nice gentlemen. In the South, some of the wealthiest, most polished men were in the ranks as they were fighting for the cause, not the pay. Their cause was states' rights and most of them were opposed to secession until Lincoln called for troops which caused them to rush to the front and fight for their homes.

I forget I am writing about incidents of the war and I must keep to that. At the time I had Mr. Flint for a home guard, many other families in town had them. It was a protection to us and a great pleasure and rest for the soldiers to have a comfortable home to stay in. We had them over two months. There was a pretty, respectable girl who fell in love with one of the guards and her father sent him back to camp. Her grandmother lived near the camp and she later went to visit her. They arranged to meet and he got a minister to marry them. In two months the army moved toward Richmond and it was then that she found from some soldiers who knew him that he already had a wife and children in the North.

Her father would not let her come back home but after the surrender her mother was taken ill and kept calling for her daughter. At last Dr. Walls told the father that he could not give them much hope for his wife's recovery unless he sent for the daughter to come and nurse her. He said there was no one else around that they could trust and he need not speak to her while she was there. He also said she could leave after his wife recovered. Doctor told me if she got home she would never leave and so it was.

It was no wonder that the people of the Valley hated Sheridan. From the time he first took control of Winchester they went into the houses and took what they wanted. They came in our house and took everything they could find to eat. I told them they were taking all I had and that I could not get anything after it was gone. They said that was too bad because Sheridan had told them never to go hungry but to help themselves. He said he wanted to make the Valley so poor that a crow would have to carry his rations when he flew over.

They came very near doing it when they began falling back from Winchester. They burned every barn, every hay stack, and every wheat field for twenty miles on either side of the Pike. We could stand in our door and see fires in all directions, 10 or 15 at one time. They cut all the bearing fruit trees and carried the branches over their shoulders, eating the fruit off of them as they marched along. I had several damson trees full of ripe fruit and they cut off the limbs and took them all. They ruined our gardens, what they were not able to take, they destroyed. There never was an army in the world as well provisioned as the Federal Army. At the same time, our men were suffering for the mere necessities of life and were literally starving.

It was true that Sheridan had said that the only way to subdue the South was to starve them. They came near doing it as only a few farmers who lived far from the Pike, where the army seldom passed, were able to harvest any crops. The Yanks took all the horses that were able to work and they never left any cow that gave milk. They would drive the cows along with them as far as they could and then they would butcher them. Oh, well, what is the use of writing about all this, it only makes me feel badly.

They shot all the hogs they could find and sometimes they would not even take the meat. One morning I was in my kitchen and I knew the army was passing by but the way they were moving I did not think they would stop to pillage. I had been working with my meat and I could not take it down. A Yank came by my door with a ham and I asked him where he got it and he said, "Out of your meat house." He said it was the last piece because the other boys had got the rest. I told him I would go to his captain and get a stop put to this stealing. "Go ahead," he said, "he is the one who told us to help ourselves." He said, "I smell fresh bread and I want some of that too." I told him there was some in the oven but it was not done yet. By this time the kitchen was full and they opened the oven door and they walked off with all the half-baked bread.

They did not find the rest of the flour as I had set the barrel in the middle of the floor with a square board on top. Then I put a table cloth down over it with books and a lamp sitting on it. When they left, they took all my jam and jelly and the flour was all we had left.

One cool fall evening an ambulance escorted by 10 Yank soldiers stopped in front of our house. A lady and a gentleman came to the door and asked if they could stay all night. They were from Illinois and were on their way up the Valley to Rockbridge County to see their parents, as they had gone west some time before. Hearing that Sheridan had possession of the Valley, they thought they might be able to get home. When they reached Winchester, however, they found Sheridan could only give them a pass and escort as far as Newtown. As there were no horses for hire at that time, they did not know how they were going to get the additional hundred miles they still had to go.

The man had bought himself a gray suit and they talked of being sympathetic with the South as they were born in the Valley and all their relatives still lived there. Dr. Walls told them they were welcome to stay and agreed to go with them the next morning to help find some means of conveyance.

We had just finished supper and were seated in the parlor when about 20 Yankee soldiers burst through the front door. They commenced searching the house without saying a word to us. They found an old shotgun in my closet that belonged to William which they broke to pieces on the pavement in front of the house. Since most of the servants were gone then, I had hired an Englishman as a cook. When they searched the dining room, they found him hiding under the table. They knew he was the Rebel, Dr. William Walls. I told them he was my cook but they

Typical style of the 1860s. AC

laughed as they were sure they had finally captured my stepson William.

When they left they took all the men, my cook, the gentleman from Illinois and Dr. Walls. I never saw anyone more frightened than the man's wife. She cried and screamed and wished she had never left home. For my part, I was glad she had gotten a little taste of the war. The people of the Northern states knew nothing of what it was like except what they read in the papers which was usually only the accounts of the battles, and they were never correct. They had no idea of what the poor Southerners had to suffer.

I do not remember the name of the couple, but she thought I was some kind of heroine to take everything so calmly. Since I had become accustomed to it, I tried to calm her down as much as possible. I told her I expected her husband would be back before morning as they would take them to headquarters and examine them. Then when they could show proof that they were all right, they would be released. Sure enough, they all came back later that night, including my cook. They had taken about a hundred prisoners in town that night trying to find three of Stonewall's Brigade believed to have slipped in to see their families. There were several suspected spies in town who were believed to have kept Yankees informed about citizens' activities.

CHAPTER EIGHTEEN

LIFE IN A YANKEE PRISON

THE U.S. HISTORY THAT HAS BEEN WRITTEN SINCE THE WAR is not correct except for the dates. When I read it I laugh, but at the same time it makes me mad to see such lies. Most of the men who wrote it were safe at home and never smelled gun powder. As to the official records, of course they copied them the best they could and they could not be changed much. Russell, the great English reporter who was with the Northern Army at Bull Run, reported it as it was to the London papers. It so outraged the Yankees that they almost ran him out of the country. I have been told by some of the Northern Army that several papers that dared tell the truth in regard to the awful treatment of Southern prisoners were suppressed by the government.

They talk and write long accounts of Andersonville and Libby Prison in Richmond, knowing that their men were never treated with the cruelty that our poor men received at Johnson Island and Elmira, New York. I had friends in both of these prisons and I had a brother in Elmira. He will not hardly talk about how they treated the sick. Those who were not sick were vaccinated with impure virus on purpose. Many of their arms got infected and

some had to have them amputated while others died. My brother said his arm was awful and they wanted to take it off but he would not have it, he told them he would rather die. His arm was useless for a long time but that is what they wanted so if there was an exchange they could not return to active service.

They also tried to starve our men as they never had enough to eat as bad as it was. There was no excuse for that as the U.S. Government was the most well provisioned army in the world. We had nothing in the South to feed our army and the prisoners at Andersonville fared as well or better than our soldiers.

They would not exchange prisoners as they did not care how many of their men were in our prisons, they could always get more to take their place. The Germans were coming over by the thousands, all anxious to fight for money. The most cruel prison officers were Lew Wallace, Charles DeLand and B.J. Sweet. They would have our men tied by their thumbs and beaten with sticks at the slightest offense.

Andersonville. This infamous prison was the site of 13,000 deaths, most attributable to disease and starvation.

Mollie's brother, Carroll M. Hansford, was captured June 3, 1864, at the Battle of Cold Harbor. He was held a short time at Pt. Lookout, Maryland, and on June 17 was transferred to Elmira, New York. He was imprisoned there eight months which included the bitter New York winter of 1865. Of the 12,122 Confederates held at Elmira, 2,917 died, 17 escaped, and 218 were left in the hospital too sick to be sent home when the war ended.

A collection of 34 letters, both from and to Carroll Hansford while he was a prisoner have been preserved by family descendants. Although they were heavily censored, they reveal how crucial family support was to the lives of the prisoners. (For additional letters from this collection, see Appendix B.)

Prisoners Camp
Point Lookout, Maryland
June 29th, 1864

My Dear Sister: (Vic.)

I wrote to you from this place about two weeks ago and have been looking anxiously for an answer for several days. I was taken prisoner on the 3rd of June and got here on the 17th. Pete is safe as he was not well and was not in the fight. Brooks was not captured or hurt and Grant was not in the fight, being unwell at the time.

I am in a bad fix here having no money and no clothes except those I have on. I am almost compelled to have money but hate to ask Father for it. I wish you would see Stephen Capehart and see if he would loan me 25 or 30 dollars and if he does, please send it immediately.

My love to father, Cint and Charley.
Send to Co. K, 12th Div. Miss. V.F.
C. Hansford
Your Brother

Coalsmouth—July '64

My Dear Carroll

We received your letter with regret and pleasure. Regret that you are a prisoner, and pleasure that we have at last heard from you and know where you are and at least know you are not dead.

Oh, Carroll, I suppose I have an exaggerated idea of a prison, but ever since I heard that so many of the old 22nd were captured, I feel oppressed as if I were behind those prison bars.

Cousin M.A. Teays thinks Steve is dead because nothing will convince her to the contrary as you did not mention him in your letter. When you write again, mention Steve, Tom Grant, Pole N. and George Chilton. Aunt Thenie's folks are very anxious about him.

I am sending you a fine-tooth comb, use it, is my parting injunction. Give my respects to all the boys I know who are with you.
Your Sister,
Cint

Of the 12,122 Confederate prisoners held at Elmira, New York, 2,917 died, 17 escaped and 218 were left in the hospital too sick to be sent home when the war ended. LC

A censored envelope received by Carroll M. Hansford while he was imprisoned at Elmira, New York.

Since U.S. mail service did not extend into the Kanawha Valley during part of the war, steamboats were authorized to pick up prisoners mail and drop it off at Gallipolis where it could be routed through the regular U.S. Postal system. HFC

Elmira, New York
August '64

My Dear Sister:

I am getting along very well considering the fact I am in prison. The major commanding the prison appears a perfect gentlemen and treats us all very well. *(This statement was probably for the benefit of the censor.)*

There are 10 or 11 Kanawhans here but none of your acquaintances except John Simms.

I would like very much to have something good to eat as I have had nothing extra since I have been here. Most of the boys have had provisions sent from home.

Carroll M. Hansford

The following letter was written by Carroll Hansford the same day he was released from Elmira prison. The letter is a classic account of the times and portrays the mixed emotions that confronted him.

After expressing his happiness about being released, he seemed to realize while writing the letter that because of his emaciated condition his chances of making it home alive were slim. It was the middle of a cold New York winter, he was sick, without warm clothing, had little money, and was facing an uncertain trip of over seven hundred miles. Rather than play it safe by staying back in the prison hospital, he was determined to undertake the long journey even though he had little hope he would make it. Believing he would never see his family again, he proceeded to tell them all good bye.

Although there is no known record of Carroll's trip home, we do know that he made it back to Coalsmouth (now St. Albans) where he lived a long and productive life.

Prison Camp, Elmira
Feb. 15, 1865

My Dear Sister Vic.

Have just received your letter and it was just in time for I leave here today for the south. I am truly glad to leave for I am heartily tired of this place. Indeed I do not think I could have lived much longer if I stayed here. I expect the trip will be a pretty hard one for me as I am very weak but I intend to try it as it can't do more than kill me.

I wrote to Cint several days ago and to Charley yesterday and I also wrote to Cousin Dep. If I don't make it, remember me to all my friends and bid them good bye for me. Give my love to Father, Cint, and Charley. I hope you will all be kind to our father for he has seen trials and troubles enough in this world. And as in all probability you will never see or hear from me again, I bid you all a long, long good bye.

C.M. Hansford

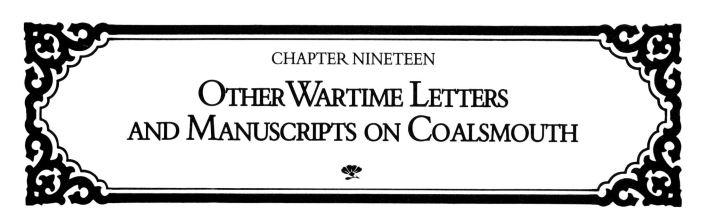

CHAPTER NINETEEN
OTHER WARTIME LETTERS AND MANUSCRIPTS ON COALSMOUTH

MOLLIE'S COUSIN, STEPHEN P. CAPEHART (1832-1905), *wrote an article titled "Coalsmouth" which was published in the West Virginia Historical Magazine, Vol. 5-1, January 1905. Since it gives an additional view of the war and its effects on the neighborhood, portions of the paper are included here.*

Coalsmouth: by Stephen P. Capehart

In 1859, political clouds began to hover over our peaceful village and everything looked dark and gloomy. I was one of those who wanted to save the country by trying to elect Bell and Everett who stood for the Constitution and our Union. The Democrats divided, however, which got Mr. Lincoln elected. Then the trouble began and it kept up for four long years.

In our town there was strife, neighbor against neighbor, and in some cases son against the father. The times were awful—soldiers would shoot at citizens just for fun.

No. 1 Lock on Coal River near the south end of "B" Street, St. Albans, about 1876.

These were anything but balmy days for Coalsmouth. From the beginning of the war there were no ministers of the Gospel, and there were no doctors. The soul and body were left to their chances, but there was not a death in the village during the four years. After it was all over and business got back to normal, the doctors and preachers returned and people began to sicken and die.

Before the war, the Coal River was made navigable by a series of locks and dams constructed by the Coal River Navigation Company. They shipped cannel coal from Peytona in Boone County to New Orleans until the war started. The company president was William S. Rosecrans who later became a Yankee general. In 1861 a fleet of loaded barges was tied up at Lock No. 1. When General Wise evacuated the Valley, he ordered them scuttled. The coal washed downstream and was gathered and used by the town's people for many years.

Mollie Hansford and the Wife of General Ord

When Mollie was about 14, she had a girlfriend in Coalsmouth who was destined to become involved in the Civil War in a very strange and amazing way. Years later, Mollie wrote about it in one of her journals. However, there was even more to the story than Mollie knew. With the availability of modern research material, additional facts have now been added to the remarkable story of the woman who once lived in Coalsmouth.

I went to a political outing with my father that was held on Coal River. There I met Mary Thompson who had come to Coalsmouth to live with her grandmother, Mrs. Philip R. Thompson, after her mother died in Charleston. She was about my age and we became good friends until she moved back to Charleston after her father, Robert Thompson, remarried. I afterwards heard that the family moved to California where Mary later married General Ord of the U.S. Army.

What Mollie never knew was that Robert Thompson, Mary's father, married the second time to Elizabeth P. Early of Buffalo in Putnam County. She was the daughter of Colonel Joab Early and a sister of Jubal Early who became a distinguished Confederate general. Therefore, Mary Thompson Ord's husband was a Major General in the Union Army while her stepmother's brother was a Major General in the Confederate Army.

It should also be noted that Mary Thompson Ord was the same woman that Mary Todd Lincoln unjustly accused in public of having an affair with her husband, President Lincoln.

Robert A. Thompson, Mary's father, was born in Culpeper County February 14, 1805. He attended the University of Virginia, studied law, was admitted to the bar in 1826, and began law practice in Charleston. He was a member of the Virginia State Senate, 1839-46, and a member of the U.S. House of Delegates, 1847-49. He moved to San Francisco, California, in

mementoes of the school to send home. At the time VMI was burned, Cooney Ricketts was enrolled there. Cunningham was also in the third Battle of Winchester when Colonel George S. Patton was killed on the opposing line.

The John Cunningham letters were first published in the St. Albans Historical Society Journal, 1986 Fall Edition. Special recognition is extended to the editor, Dorothy Locke, for her excellent documentation of the Cunningham material. For collecting and preserving these valuable papers, Mary Ann Lewis of St. Albans also deserves a special commendation.

Lexington, Rockbridge Co., Va.
Sunday 12, June, 1864

My Dear Wife,
Last Thursday I wrote you from Staunton. The morning following, we took up our line of march for this place and covered 24 miles.

* * * * *

This morning I am seeing the Va. Military Institute in flames. All the public buildings connected with the institution are being destroyed. Quite a large number of guns and small arms were captured. Lexington is quite a beautiful place. I have no time to write all the particulars. The casualties in the Regt. are two men wounded viz T.N. Hogg and Wm. Harris, both of Co. B, they are not dangerously hurt.

Tell Mrs. Overshiner there are no casualties in Co. G., Capt. Young's Co., that I know of. I saw Mr. O. this morning. Love to Father and Mother. Kiss Eva for me. God bless you all
Your affectionate husband,
John S. Cunningham

Camp Piatt — June 30th
I have not had any means to send you this until now. I send by Chaplain Harper this small rough bundle containing a book brought from the Va. Mil. Inst. together with a magnet. Please take care of them for me as momentoes of that place.
Your affectionate husband,
J.S. Cunningham

1853. He was appointed to the committee to settle California land claims in 1853 and was appointed reporter for the California Supreme Court in 1870. He died in San Francisco on August 31, 1876.

Civil War Letters of John S. Cunningham

These letters are extremely important to the overall history of the Civil War in Coalsmouth. John S. Cunningham was one of the few Union soldiers from the neighborhood. He was an officer in the 13th West Virginia Infantry, the same regiment that Sergeant Griffith was in when he was mortally wounded at Cedar Creek.

In several of the letters to his wife, John Cunningham mentioned John Overshiner and Captain John Young. They were both in the same company as Sergeant Griffith and were witnesses on his mother's pension claim. John Overshiner also drew the picture of the Coal River covered bridge included in another chapter. Captain Young was from Putnam County.

Although there were only a few Union families in Coalsmouth, they managed to coexist with their Rebel neighbors during and after the war. However, Mollie and Victoria completely ignored them in their writings, since they never mentioned Yankees families who lived in Coalsmouth.

In one of his letters, Lieutenant Cunningham wrote that he had seen the Virginia Military Institute burning, and he had

Head Quarters 13th Regt. West Va. Vol Inf
Camp near Hall Town, Va., Aug. 25th, 1864

My Dear Wife,

Day before yesterday evening just as this regt. was ordered out on the skirmish line, I received a letter from you dated July 24th and one from Father dated Aug. 2nd. They contained the first news I have had from home since I left the Valley.

* * * * *

Tell Mrs. Overshiner that I saw her husband, Capt. Young and all the company that was present last Sunday before the battle. They were then all well and since the regt. was not engaged, consequently they are still all right.

* * * * *

I send you ten thousand sweet little kisses. I know you are an excellent little wife to me. Goodbye.
Your affectionate husband,
John S. Cunningham
Adj. 13th Regt. WVVI

Included among the papers was a certificate appointing John Cunningham to the Military Order of the United States, dated August 14, 1893, four months after his death. His biography and war record were contained in this notice and warrant inclusion as part of Coalsmouth's Civil War history.

John Sharp Cunningham
Born at North Orange, N.J. Jan. 15, 1827
Died at St. Albans, W.Va. April 22, 1893
2nd Lt. 11th W.Va. Inf. July 22, 1862
1st Lt. and Adjutant, 13th W.Va. Inf. Apr. 2, 1863
Honorably Discharged Jan. 10, 1865

Companion Cunningham graduated at Orange Academy in 1844 having made a specialty in surveying and civil engineering. After working as an engineer for several R.R. companies in New Jersey and Pa., he moved to Coalsmouth in 1858. Here he made the survey that formed the basis for the Coal River Railroad. In 1856 he married Helen Benedict, daughter of Samuel Benedict.

He took part in the following engagements during the rebellion:

1862: With the 11th Infantry — Barboursville, Va., September 8; Guyandotte, Sept. 8; Charley's Creek, Sept. 11; Hurricane Bridge, Sept. 11; Charleston, Sept. 13.

1863: With the 13th Infantry — Fayetteville, May 20-21; Raleigh C.H., May 23; Pomeroy, O., July 18; Buffington Island, July 19.

1864: Lexington, Va., June 12; Lynchburg, June 17-18; Buford's Gap, July 15; Cabletown, July 18; Winchester, July 23-24; Martinsburg, July 24; Charles Town, Aug. 21; Halltown, Aug. 24-26; Berryville, Sept. 3; Winchester, Sept. 19; Fisher's Hill, Sept. 22; Round Top Mt., Oct. 9; Cedar Creek, Oct. 13-19. After Cedar Creek he was sent to field hosp. at Winchester, thence to hosp. at Martinsburg and then to an officer's hosp. at Annapolis, Md.

In the restoration of affairs after the war, he was appointed the first superintendent of free schools for Kanawha Co. was appointed director and president of the Kanawha Board of Public Works for the improvement of the great Kanawha River with a system of sluice navigation. Several years before his death he had been President of Kanawha Co. Court.

John Cunningham, his father-in-law, Samuel Benedict, and his brother-in-law, Park Benedict, became prominent businessmen in early St. Albans. They became extensive landowners, and such names as Belvil Park, Benedict Circle, and Cunningham Memorial Park still call to mind some of their early enterprises.

General U.S. Grant's Uncle Lived in Coalsmouth

Roswell Grant was first attracted to the Kanawha Valley by William Tompkins who had married his sister, Rachael, and lived at Cedar Grove. Tompkins and Grant had both purchased farms from the old Valcoulon estate before the war. William Tompkins did not live on his portion but made it available to the Confederate forces for a training camp. Roswell Grant, who was a tanner by trade, established a tanning yard on his land. Although their nephew was a prominent Union general, both Grant and Tompkins favored the Confederate cause.

When the war started, Roswell Grant's son, Thomas, was one of the first in town to enlist in the Confederate Army. This created a situation for the Grant family that led the father to move to Kentucky until after the war. When the Confederate forces were in control of the area, Roswell Grant was harassed because his nephew was U.S. Grant, and when the Union troops took over, he was badgered because he had a son in the Rebel Army.

Mrs. Carol Quillen of St. Albans came by a letter written by Roswell Grant dated September 7, 1874, which she researched and published in the St. Albans Historical Society Journal, Spring 1974 edition. Not only did the letter contain important Grant family history, it added another chapter to the Civil War story in Coalsmouth.

Mayslick, Mason Co., Ky.
September 7, 1874

George A. Young, Esq.
Dear Sir:

I have just received yours of August 28th, also a circular inviting me to a reunion of old citizens and pioneers of Youngstown, Ohio. Nothing would have given me more pleasure than to meet you on that occasion. Had only I received a notice ten days sooner I would certainly have done so. As I am a farmer, it is impossible to leave on so short a notice.

It has brought to mind many old reminiscences. My mother died at Deerfield in 1805. My father moved to Youngstown the same year where he carried on a tannery business.

*　*　*　*　*

I left Youngstown in 1818 and went to Ravenna. Stayed there until 1820 when I went to Maysville, Ky. Finished learning my trade with my brother, Peter Grant. After following my trade for 28 years, I quit tanning and bought me a farm of 775 acres on the Kanawha River, below Charleston, the capitol of West Virginia. During the late war I was so annoyed by both armies, I rented the farm out and came here in 1862 and bought the small farm where I now live, 13 miles south of Maysville, Mason Co., Ky.
I remain, yours truly
Roswell M. Grant

Roswell Grant evidently returned to St. Albans in later years as he is buried with his wife, Jane, in the Episcopal Cemetery on College Hill.

The tombstone reads:

Roswell M. Grant	*1800-1888*
Jane E.	*1804-1857*

Battle flag of 13th West Virginia Infantry. WEST VIRGINIA CULTURE AND HISTORY COLLECTION

EPILOGUE

A FEW MONTHS AFTER THE WAR, MOLLIE'S SECOND CHILD, Mary Adalade, "Mamie," was born, and she settled down to the peaceful life of a housewife and mother. However, this tranquil existence was not to last. A short time later, Dr. Walls died suddenly and left her alone with two small children. As soon as the estate was settled, which amounted to little after the war, Mollie decided to move back to Coalsmouth to live near her relatives.

In 1875 Mollie was married to Major Vincent R. Rust, a widower, who had been her school teacher when they were both much younger. After they were married, Mollie and her two children, Hansford and Mamie, went to live at Major Rust's estate, Locust Grove, at the present site of Rock Branch in Putnam County.

Major Rust had a daughter, Cathrine "Catty" Rust, whose mother had died several years before. The children adjusted amazingly well, and in a short time a warm and devoted family emerged. By 1878 Hansford and Mamie Walls were enrolled in Coalsmouth High School, formerly Shelton College, and they boarded with relatives in Coalsmouth. Catty Rust and her stepsister, Mamie, later attended Wesleyan Female Institute in Staunton, Virginia. At the same time, Hansford went to live with his half brother, Dr. William Walls, in Baltimore and attended the Medical School at the University of Maryland. After graduation in 1881, he returned home and married his stepsister, Catty Rust, and began practice in Poca, West Virginia. He later practiced in Pratt and in Nitro, West Virginia, where he died in 1937.

After the war, Victoria Hansford remained at Coalsmouth where she continued to manage the household for her father and brothers. She had also begun a courtship by mail with a tall, handsome officer she had seen riding by her uncle's house at Paint Creek. She had refugeed there with others before the Battle of Scary, and she was still there when the Confederate Army passed by on their way out of the Valley. She was so taken with the young soldier she saw that day, she asked if anyone knew his name. Luckily some-

one did. He was Lieutenant Thomas A. Teays of Chapman's Battery from Monroe County. Although there are no details available, Victoria must have been persistent and determined to win the heart of Tom Teays, as it was not until 12 years later they were happily married at Coalsmouth on June 5, 1873.

Victoria and Thomas Teays acquired the old Teays Tavern and after remodeling it, they continued to operate it as an inn. After 1876, they turned the old building into a residence that was occupied by family members until 1930.

Victoria and her husband had two children: a son, C.R. "Capt" Teays, and Maria, who married Joseph S. Barker. Mrs. "Vicky," as she was affectionately called, became a devoted worker in her church and community. She was a charter member of the Coalsmouth Baptist Church, 10-year president of the Women's Christian Temperance Union, and regent of the United Daughters of the Confederacy.

In one of her addresses before a UDC group, Victoria expressed her wartime feelings:

"Oh, how we prized their letters that came through the underground railroad. They had been written without restraint by loving hands and had been borne to us by friends staunch and true. They were from our boys who were true to their homes, true to their loved ones, and true to the South that we loved so well.

"Looking back, I remember how they labored, and how they fought, and how they suffered and died. My heart grows sick and my eyes grow dim at the thought that it was all in vain. We have been true to their memory, true to the Southland, and true to the 'Lost Cause' for which they died. May all women of the South ever be true to them and honor their graves."

Tragedy struck the Hansford family in Coalsmouth in 1875 when their father, Major John Hansford, was killed. Only a few yards from his home, he was hit by a train while walking across the railroad trestle over Coal River. The accident drew considerable attention since the railroad had been completed only a few months earlier. (See Appendix C.)

Mollie's husband, Vincent R. Rust, died in 1894, and she continued to live at Locust Grove with her son and his family until her death in 1900. On January 1, 1899, a year before she died, she made the following entry in her last journal:

"It is a dark gloomy day and as I sit here alone in my room I look back over my life and realize how many New Years' Days I have enjoyed that are now passed and gone forever. I can but think of my neglected opportunities, the misused privileges, and the mistakes of my eventful life. These things cannot be changed but are now only vain regrets.

I thank my Heavenly Father for his many blessings as I bid the old year adieu. I welcome the New Year with earnest prayers that I may make better use of my remaining days and try to do more for His Glory and the good of those around me."

APPENDICES

APPENDIX A: LOCAL BATTLE CASUALTIES

	NORTH	SOUTH
First Kernstown, Mar. 23, 1862	590	718
Front Royal, May 23, 1862	904	50
First Winchester, May 25, 1862	3,000	400
Second Winchester, June 14, 1863	4,443	269
Second Kernstown, July 23, 1864	1,185	600
Third Winchester (Opequon), Sept. 19, 1864	5,018	3,921
Fishers Hill, Sept. 22, 1864	528	1,235
Cedar Creek, Oct. 19, 1864	5,665	2,910
Totals	**21,333**	**10,153**
Combined Total Casualties		**31,485**

Note: Losses taken from The Civil War Dictionary—Mark M. Boatner III, Lt. Col., U. S. Army

APPENDIX B: PRISONER OF WAR CORRESPONDENCE

LETTERS TO AND FROM CARROLL M. HANSFORD, BROTHER OF MOLLIE WALLS, WHILE HE WAS IMPRISONED AT ELMIRA, NEW YORK.

Coalsmouth, Aug. 24, 1864
Dear Carroll,

This is the 5th letter I have written you and I am almost discouraged as you have never received any of them. Are they too long or what is the matter? We girls have been very busy fixing up a box for you, John Simms, Ned Davenport and some things to give to the destitute ones of the Kanawha boys. We had pieces finished and would have sent them this week had it not been for the order prohibiting anything more being sent. We were all so disappointed for we had talked and thought of nothing else for weeks. Twas worse than planning a Methodist supper.

Why don't you write often, don't despair. We have your clothes and may be able to send them yet. Lin has made you a fancy shirt and we have drawers and such nice socks for you.

Did you know Capt. Irwin Lewis was in Ft. Delaware?

My respects to all the Rebs
Your Little Sis

Elmira, New York
August 20
Dear Vick:

Since the letter you wrote was over length, I received only your signature and the envelope. You must be careful in the future and write only one page on letter paper. You must not say anything that is contraband, nothing about politics, war, or religion. If you do, the authorities will not let the letter be delivered.

There has been quite a change in the program here since my last letter. Prisoners are not allowed to receive clothing or provisions from their friends owing to an order from Washington. The same order also prohibits the sutler to sell anything except tobacco, stationery, and stamps, but nothing to eat. So you see it will be of no use to send me anything as they will not let me have it.

Your Brother
C. M. Hansford

Mouth of Scary
August 24, 1864

My Dear Brother:

I learn through the newspapers—which never lie, but which I hope they do in this case—that prisoners will not be permitted to receive any more boxes, clothing, etc. I am truly sorry as the girls have a number of articles which they propose sending to those of their acquaintances who are in great need of such things.

Vic will write to you soon. Let me advise you while a prisoner, not to give way to despondency. I do not doubt that it kills more imprisoned men than any disease. Never sigh when you can laugh. Take exercise and take the best care of yourself as possible. By the way, did I tell you I am teaching school at Scary? My health is much better than when you saw me last. Write often as I am always anxious to hear from you.

Your Aff. Brother
Charles

Prison Camp
Sept. 16th, '64

My Dear Sister: (Vic)

I am sorry you did not send the box you had ready because they are letting clothes come through.

Vic, when you write again I want to know what has become of O. J. Wilson. Geo. Chilton told me he thought he went home last spring. If he is, let me know what account he gives of himself.

By the way, what has become of Uncle Alvah, give him my best respects. My respects also to Cousin James Teays. My regards also to Stephen Capehart and family and Uncle Wilson and family. These in particular, and all my other friends in general.

My love to Father, Cint and Charles. I'm sorry times are so hard with you but God will surely watch over and keep you all.

Your Aff. Brother
Carroll

Coalsmouth
Oct. 31, 1864

My Dear Brother,

First I wanted to ask you about a package I put in your last box. Ruffner wrote to us about a young man who was sick, a Mr. Caldwell by name who he said was very friendless and destitute. So when we were making up the box I put in a package of underclothing, tobacco, paper and stamps for him. Now I wonder if he ever received it. I fear more likely he is dead. He was from near White Sulphur Springs. Make some inquiries and let me know as I took such an interest in sending the things to him as I wanted him to get them.

Kit, I sent a little coffee and some extract. It will make the coffee go twice as far if you will put in a piece the size of a chestnut in a half gallon of coffee. I also sent a little tea and white sugar to use if you should get sick. After you use your blackberries, the can may be used to make your tea in.

I also sent a few potatoes but could send much more if we had room in the box. Write soon.

Your Sister
Vic

The Mr. Caldwell referred to could have most likely been Archibald Caldwell who enlisted at White Sulphur Springs, captured at Winchester 9-19-1864, died 2-10-1927 in Craig Co., Va., age 83. However, the History of The 22nd Va. Inf. by Terry D. Lowry lists 18 known former members of the regiment with the surname of Caldwell, most of whom were from Craig Co., Va.

Prison Camp "Elmira"

My Dear Sister:

Your letter and last box have been received. I wrote to Charley saying it had arrived. I can't imagine what keeps my letters so long on the way. It only takes yours four or five days to reach me while mine are nearly as many weeks on the way.

I wish I could be exchanged as I have been no doubt a great source of worry and expense to you all. But I hope you will bear with me as I intend to be as little trouble as possible to you all.

I will certainly keep and prize highly your gift of the Bible as well as the principles it teaches, especially since it is a gift from my beloved sister.

Your Brother
Carroll

Mouth of Scary
Oct. 31st, 1864

My Dear Brother:

We are all well at home. Father and the girls are getting things together for another box. It will probably take some time though as things to put in it are getting a little difficult to come by.

Learned from your letter to Cint that you are unwell—hope you are improved by now. I heard yesterday of the death of Tom Grant who was at Pt. Lookout. I have a faint hope the report is unfounded. 'Twould be a terrible blow to his sisters.

Your Brother
Chas. V. Hansford

The report of the death of Tom Grant was true. It should be noted that he was a first cousin of General U. S. Grant of the Union Army.

Coalsmouth, Nov. 11th, 1864

My Dear Brother:

I went to Charleston last week and got some material to make you some clothes. The girls came and we finished them. Now they say I can't start your box until I get a written order from Maj. Colt. I want you to get an order as soon as you can for me to send the following articles: a pair of pants, an overcoat, a hat, an undershirt, a pair of socks and a blanket. Don't wait a day until you send the "permit" as they call it. The express agent in Cincinnati won't accept any box unless an order is with it.

We thought an overcoat would keep you warmer than a jacket. I have sent you money twice and Charley has once or twice. Did you ever get it?

Your Sister
Cint

Kanawha, Va., Nov. 15, 1864

My Dear Cousin:

I was at your father's when your first letter came and we all began right then making clothes for you. Have you received a box by now?

Cousin Monroe is a prisoner at Pt. Lookout where you were first. If there is any Kanawha boys of my acquaintance with you, give my best love to them.

You must write to me dear cousin. I fear you will not spend a very pleasant winter but hope for the best.

With many prayers for your safety and a speedy return home,

I am ever your affectionate cousin.

Kate Hansford

Monroe Hansford was a member of the 8th Va. Cav. and was captured at Winchester 9-19-1864, died 1908 and is buried in Spring Hill Cemetery, Huntington, W. Va.

The following letter to Carroll "Kit" Hansford is from his cousin Stephen T. Teays. Born in Coalsmouth, now St. Albans, enlisted in the 22nd Va. Inf. at Charleston, captured at Winchester, Va. 9-19-65, prisoner at Pt. Lookout, MD., took oath and was released 2-25-65. Was a merchant in St. Albans, City Treasurer 1896, died 1901, buried at Teays Hill Cemetery.

Point Lookout, Md.
Nov. 16, 1864

Friend Kit:

I have just received your letter and glad to know you are well. I feel a great deal better than I did when I first came here. I was very sorry to hear of the death of poor Will Lewis—did you hear what was the matter with him and where he died?

You spoke of my appetite, I believe that the food or the water will get me yet if I stay here. Lewis Hawkins died a few days since and also Eddy Cox.

Well Judge, I feel like John Well's old horse Jack and you know how that was. Our sutler has played out on us and that makes times about right. You must write often.

My respects to all.

Yours truly,
S. T. Teays

The report on Will Lewis' death was false as he is listed as transferring to the 8th Va. Cav., June 1862, was captured, took the oath, and was released 12-6-64. Lewis Hawkins born in Craig Co., Va. was captured at Fisher's Hill, Va., 9-22-64. Died at Pt. Lookout, Md. of typhoid fever 11-6-64. The only information available on E. Cox, Co. H., 22nd Inf. lists him as being left in hospital at Winchester, Va. in 1864.

Coalsmouth, Kan. Co.
Nov. 21st, 1864

Mr. C. M. Hansford:

My dear son, enclosed I remit to you herewith ten dollars to the care of Major Colt commanding the post at Elmira, New York.

From the polite attention that gentleman has paid to the boxes you have received, I hope you will receive this as well. I shall put it in the box we now send you, with an overcoat, pair pants and shirt. The girls send you a counter pen with some other things which I hope you will be allowed to receive, as I think they will not infringe on the rules of the post.

Keep in good spirits and I hope it will not be long until arrangements will be made to exchange all prisoners.
John Hansford

Coalsmouth, Nov. 19, 1864

My Dear Carroll:

Dear Brother, I hope you like the things we have sent as we have done the best we possibly could. You must not think we are setting on flower beds of ease while you are suffering in prison for indeed we are not. The very thought of your being there keeps us distressed. We will never let you suffer if we can help it.

We could have sent you something more in your last box but Mr. Sims wanted to send a small bundle for John and you know we southern people try to help each other when we can.

Cousin James got a letter from Pete Brooks the other day and he wants to take the oath and come home. This is a strong thing to do but he should not have to suffer from it. Old Mr. Brooks has already petitioned for Pete to come home. Write as soon as you can.

Your Sister
Vic

Napoleon B. "Pete" Brooks is listed in the History of The 22nd Va. Inf. by Terry Lowry as a 1st Sgt. Co. H., 22nd Inf., enlisted at Coalsmouth (St. Albans) 7-10-61. Captured at Winchester, Va. 9-19-64. Confined at Pt. Lookout, Md. Took the oath and was released 2-25-65.

Coalsmouth, Dec. 26. 1864

Dear Carroll:

We are sending you a box of eatables. Tell John Sims that we are very sorry that we could not send his sister word so she could have included something in the box for him. The river has been out of its banks and it is so muddy that it is impossible to get about at all. I expect John will be disappointed but I reckon you will divide with him anyway.

I heard from Sister Mollie the other day for the first time since you were captured. She is well but says she feels like she has been forsaken since all the boys she knew from over here are all gone now. Said she had seen Milt and Nick Hansford and all the boys of the 22nd when they were at Newtown several times last summer.

I was sorry your coat was so large but I guess it will keep you warm anyway.

Your Sister
Cint

Coalsmouth, Dec. 26, 1864

My Dear Brother,

We sent you the box we promised which contained such Sunday articles as coffee, sugar, canned fruit, cakes, pickles, sausage, souse, dried beef, and butter. We could not send the box on Christmas Eve as there was no boat, but hope you will get it soon after New Years.

We also sent tobacco and there are many other things we could send but the box takes so long to get there that they would spoil.

Mrs. Simms would have liked to send her brother something in the box but there was no room, so you will have to invite him to dine with you. We are all very well and send you much love.

Your Sister
Vic

Coalsmouth, Jan. 1, 1865

Dear Carroll,

It is New Years Day and I think I cannot use my time better than writing to you. It is mighty cold here now, my fingers are so cold I can hardly hold my pen. I keep thinking if its cold here it must be awfully cold up in the north where you are. The snow is six inches deep, splendid for sleigh riding but no boys to sleigh ride with.

We spent a sad dull Christmas. Somehow the egg nog and cake did not taste like it used to. Our frantic attempts to laugh and have fun generally would end up with sad talk about our friends who are prisoners.

Will Lewis has come in and given himself up. I have not seen him as he said he intended to steer clear of Coalsmouth. I don't know why.

Write soon.

Your Sister
Cint

Coalsmouth, Jan. 4, 1865

Dear Brother,

I was truly pained to hear you had been so ill and hope by the help of things sent you you will be well soon.

I received a letter from Peter yesterday. He is still trying to get home but I do not believe he will make it. Tis getting quite fashionable to "quit" and go home. I only wonder that more of those in prison are not trying to "turn their swords into plow shares."

We sent you about six pounds of dog-leg tobacco. Hope you may live long enough to use it all.

Your Aff. Brother
C. V. Hansford

Prison Camp, Elmira,
Jan. 14, 1865

Dear Brother,

The box and money were duly received for which I repeat my thanks. The sugar, coffee and especially butter have been a great help to me. I cannot get another permit for eatables as they are given at the discretion of the "Surgeon." By the way, tell Vic that the souse was spoiled but the sausage was very good indeed and although I am not entirely recovered from my illness I ventured to try several messes of it and I think it did me good.

I am aware of the doings of the boys at Pt. Lookout but I don't think they will gain much from it.

Your Aff. Brother
Carroll M. Hansford

Coalsmouth, Jan. 15, 1865

Dear Carroll,

When we heard you were sick and could not hardly eat anything we wished we had sent you more tea, sugar and nice bread. I dreamed you were so sick, oh, my brother, what would I give if you could be home once more.

Everybody is asking if you ever say anything about coming home and taking the oath. I have never seen Will Lewis, he won't come around Coalsmouth for fear we will snub him. But four years of hard fighting cannot be marked out in my mind. All the boys that come home out of prison we feel have suffered all they can bear and we will never say naught against them. But do not think for one minute that I have changed for I am stronger set in my own views than ever.

Cint

Prison Camp, Elmira
Feb. 2, 1865

My Dear Brother.

I have nothing to write about only the same old story of a bad health report. I have very little hope of ever recovering my health so long as I remain in prison. But as I'm not exactly prepared to shuffle off just yet, I intend to try to keep alive by taking the best possible care of myself.

You must not suppose by what I say that I am confined to a hospital. I have never been there yet and don't intend to be as long as I am able to keep up. I have an appetite like a sawmill but I dare not indulge it. I can eat nothing with safety but bread, tea or coffee.

If you could send me a little money I'd be so thankful as I am just out.

Your Brother
Carroll M. Hansford

A MEMORIUM TO JOHN HANSFORD

The County Court held for Kanawha County, at the Court House thereof on the 25th day of November, A.D. 1876. It has been announced to the Court that on Tuesday the 10th day of October, 1876, John Hansford, one of the Magistrates of Kanawha County, was killed at St. Albans, being struck by the Express train of the C&O RR, on the bridge across Coal River.

The Court desires to take some official notice of this sad event and do accordingly unanimously adopt the following, as an expression of esteem, for the man, and in honor of his memory:

The members of this Court have heard with deep regret of the sudden and painful death of Mr. John Hansford, the Senior Magistrate of Kanawha County. For a period beginning at a time beyond the memory of most of those who are now discharging the duties of the Magistracy of the county, he has been an active and honored member of our body commanding the respect and esteem of all. He was the living link which bound this Court so lately, made a part of our judicial system to the time of the far past, when the many worthy men who filed the positions which we occupy, administered the affairs of our County with such unusual acceptance to all.

His long experience had made him especially familiar with the varied and difficult duties which evolve upon a Magistrate, and the fact that he lived in the same community, at nearly the same plot for more than fifty years, without an enemy, or without reproach, bears witness to the impartiality and justice of his dealings with his fellowman, both socially, and as a neighbor and friend. He was the friend of peace, the legal adviser of the neighborhood, and his judicial powers were often used to arrest strife and to settle controversy, as to decide impartially when peaceful settlement was found unpracticable.

That his earthly career should have been so violently terminated is painful to us as it must have been sorrowing to his family, but it affords some consolation to all who honored and loved him, to believe that the stroke which deprived him of life was so sudden and severe as to have left him no consciousness of pain.

He was an humble man; without ambition save to deserve well of man and of his God. He was courteous and obliging to all, yet sufficiently firm to yield nothing but fairness and equitable dealing demanded he should maintain. God spared him to a good old age and though his usefulness has been manifested in no large sphere, he has "done well his part." Ours is the reward of his good example.

For ourselves, and in behalf of the Magistracy of this County, we express our sympathy with his family and friends, and to leave some monument of the high and honorable position which he so long held as a member of this body; it is hereby ordered that the Clerk of this Court do enter this paper upon the record as a part of the proceedings of this Court: That the papers of this city be requested to publish these p½roceedings, etc. That in honor of our departed associate, we do now adjourn until Monday morning next, at 10 o'clock A.M.

J. S. Quarrier, Cl'k.,
Kanawha County Court

ROLL OF BUFFALO GUARDS.

Mustered as Va. State Troops, May 13, 1861, Buffalo, Va. Afterward Co. A, 36 Va. Reg. Confederate Vol, under Col. John McCausland, (afterwards Gen. John McCausland) that left Kanawha Valley about July 24th, 1861, under Gen. H. A. Wise, when he fell back to the White Sulphur Springs, Greenbrier Co., Va.

Captain—Fife, Wm. E., (w)
1st Lieutenant—B. B. Sterrett, (w)
2d Lieutenant—Andrew J. Burford.
1st Sergeant—Wm. L. Bryan.
2d Sergeant—Wm. H. Peck, (w)
1st Corpal—L. J. Timms.
2d Corpal—Thos. H. Harvey, (w)
3rd Corpal—B. R. George.

PRIVATES

Alexander, Sam'l T.
Bryan, Rees E., (w)
Burch, Geo. W.
Bronaugh, Edward A.
Bronaugh, Chas. E., (d)
Brown, Wm. W.
Bailey, Geo., (s w)
Bowles, Jerry.
Brooks, Thos. W., (s)
Byrne, R. V., (s)
Craig, Clark.
Claughton, Wm. F.
Collins, Jno. O., (s)
Chapman, Wm. M. (s)
Deem, Sam. P.
Davis, Jno., (s)
Davis, Hen. C., (s)
Eskew, Dorsal.
Eskew, Casey.
Farrer, Democracy.
Fry, Wm. H.
Foresinger, Albert D. C., (s)
Foresinger, George, (s w)
Giles, Sam. W.
George, Andrew F.
Goings, Sam.
Harmon, Edmond.
Handley, Monroe.
Horn, Christopher.

Hogg, Henry H.
Henson, Wm. P.
Jones, Bird L., (k)
Legue, Wm. G., (k)
Legue, Simeon.
Meeks, Wm. L.
Morgan, Wm. S., (k)
McCoy, Sam. A.
McCown, Henry M.
Newman, I. V.
Newmire, A., (d)
Drummer—Neal, Hugh F.
Fifer—Neal, Jno. H.
Norvel, John (Snell)
Peck, Isaac.
Parmer, J. D., (s k)
Rait, Thos., (s)
Shank, Chas. E.
Sterrett, Sam. A.
Smith, E. A. E.
Staton, Simon C., (w)
Samuels, Dan, (s)
Samuels, Wm., (s d)
Samuels, A. B., (s w)
Samuels, Hugh, (s w)
Townsend, Paul, (s)
Wyatt, Jno. D., (d)
Wood, Jno. H.
Woods, Joseph.
Wallace, Luke T.
Watkins, Andrew J.
Withers, E. D.
Wells, Nicholas, (s k)

---

k—Killed.
w—Wounded.
d—Died.
s.—Sweeney's Company who disbanded and joined this company.

This Company had many recruits from Kanawha Valley and other parts of the country afterwards.

APPENDIX E: REMINISCENCES OF ALVA HANSFORD
(1805-1886)

A PAPER DICTATED IN THE YEAR 1884 TO WILLIAM H. ED-WARDS, AT COALBURG, W. VA., KANAWHA COUNTY, AND READ BEFORE THE WEST VIRGINIA HISTORICAL AND ANTI-QUARIAN SOCIETY, JANUARY 19, 1897, AND PUBLISHED BY THAT SOCIETY.

—NOTE ADDED BY W. H. EDWARDS:

I came to this region in 1849 to look after the Wilson survey of 85,000 acres which lay back of the river on the south side, from Cabin Creek to the Falls of Kanawha and beyond. I made the acquaintance of Mr. Alva Hansford that year and employed him more or less for several years about these lands, and especially in searching for coal seams on them. The first dozen years, and to the time of his death, I saw much of him. He was the most expert hand at discovering and tracing coal seams I have ever known, and he was, during many years after 1850, employed by other land owners in that line. He first opened on Paint Creek and traced for miles the great seam known as "The Coalburg Seam." Also, he discovered the Cannel Coal seam on Paint Creek with no more of a clue than a small piece of Cannel coal found at the base of the mountain. This seam is exposed nowhere and is covered by fully ten feet of earth; so that I count Mr. Hansford's discovery as a very great feat.

Mr. Hansford never married, nevertheless, he was ex-ceedingly fond of ladies' society and was a favorite with them. In fact, he was a beau to the mothers, daughters, and granddaughters as they grew up. I asked why he never married and he replied that he made up his mind when quite a young man that he would never marry. He said that in the families of his uncles, the more children, the more trouble. His daughters would be sure to marry men whom he did not like because of their bad habits and the sons would probably do no better. As it was, he had been happy and he did not regret it.

He built himself a small house at Coalsmouth, on the Kanawha River about 1850 and resided there alone, but was always ready to leave when business called; and to stay away as long as necessary. His brother John lived close by and nephews and nieces settled in the neighborhood. He died 22nd September 1886, aged 81 years, and was buried in the family burying ground, at Crown Hill, by the side of his parents and several brothers. Of the twelve children of John and Jane Morris Hansford, but one survived Alva, Marshall, who died in 1891.

EDITOR'S NOTE: *Alva Hansford also made two trips to Missouri, the first one in 1823 when he was 18 and second in 1826. Both trips were made in boats that he had built with his own hands.*

LISTED IN ORDER: House, name, occupation (if any), age, place of birth

308 – KIDD
William W., laborer, 60, VA
Mary A, 40, VA
Giles H., 18, VA
William, 15, VA
Sarah A., 14, VA
Mary M., 11, VA

309 – SATTES
Charles K, farmer, 54, Bavaria
Henry, 16, VA
John, 12, VA
James, 2, VA
Lethe, 39, VA
PORTER
Martinette (female), 13, VA
DINKLE
Fredrick, master carpenter, 44, Wurtenburg

310 – FORD
Alonzo, boatman, 39, VA
Susan, 38, VA
Elias F., 11, VA
Richard, 8, VA
John H., 7, VA
Susan, 4, VA
Emily L., 4 mo., VA
LEWIS
Virginia, 16, IA
America, 14, IA

311 – BEARD
Charles, farmer, 45, VA
Harriet (OGBURN), 31, VA
George, 10, VA
Charles, 5, VA
Alice, 3, VA
Sara H., 1, VA
OGBURN
Staton (?), laborer, 68, VA
Nancy, 62, VA

312 – LOFTUS
Pamelia, 45, VA
Margaret J., 21, VA
Sarah, 17, VA
Thomas J., 10, NC
Adeline, 7, NC

313 – GRASS
George W, laborer, 35, VA
Sarah M. (KIDD), 26, VA
William A., 6, VA
Ellen E., 4, VA
unnamed male, 2, VA

314 – WILSON
Charles D., farmer, 45, VA
Mary, 40, NY
Hannah E., 15, VA
Mary A., 8, VA
Martha J., 9 mo., VA
WILSON

John S., farmer, 48, KY
WELLS
John, farm laborer, 30, VA

315 – BARNETT
Nelly, farmer, 66, VA
William, laborer, 24, VA
Sally, 26, VA
Harrison, laborer, 22, VA

316 – BARNETT
John H., lumberman, 30, VA
Minerva, 31, VA
Jane, 5, VA
Elliott F., 1, VA
Mary, 1 mo., VA

317 – GROVES
Perry, carpenter, 43, VA
Mildred (SHARROCKS), 33, VA
George W., apprentice, 20, VA
James R., apprentice, 18, VA
Charles T., apprentice, 16, VA
Elizabeth E., apprentice (?), 12, VA
Ann E., 10, VA
Laura E., 8, VA
Lellia E. (female), 6, VA
John S., 4, VA
Frances (female), 1, VA

318 – RUSSEL
Meredith, laborer, 25, VA
Sarah J. (PARSONS), 22, VA
Lelia B., 1, VA
Peyton, farmer, 65, VA
Anna, 53, VA
William H., laborer, 26, VA
Elizabeth, 16, VA
Arilda, 15, VA
James, 12, VA
Anderson (male), 11, VA
(Peyton RUSSALL married Ann CHILDERS 20 Feb 1828.)

319 – BRYANT
William, farmer, 26, VA
Mary (CHANDLER?), 22, VA
KING
William R., mulatto, 6, VA

320 – DAVIS
Baxter M., (L?), laborer, 39, VA
Virginia (SMOOT), 32, NC
Mary J., 14, VA
Eliphalet (?) (male), 13, VA
Maria, 11, VA

321 – BRYANT
Andrew, farmer, 60, VA
Dicey, 51, VA
Thomas, laborer, 24, VA
Andrew J., laborer, 22, VA
Lilburn J. (male), laborer, 20, VA

Dicey, 15, VA
HOOVER
Franklin, shoemaker, 26, VA
Lausetta, 16, VA
Dicey C., 4 mo., VA

322 – GENTRY
Harman H., farmer, 55, VA
Maria, 21, VA
Sarah, 19, VA
Mary, 14, VA
Marjery, 9, VA

323 – HENLEY
Edward M., farmer, 31
Chloe, 26
Mary F., 3
Grey A. (Orey?) (male), 1
HENLY
William, carpenter, 29
Woodson, laborer, 17
Charles, mechanic, 27
James H., 6

324 – CARPENTER
Joseph, farmer, 61, VA
Ann, 49, VA
Morris, laborer, 22, VA
Harvey, laborer, 20, VA
Eliza A., 16, VA
SPURLOCK
Malinda, 4, VA

325 – CASH
Powhatan, carpenter, 46, VA
Margaret, 39, VA
James K.P., 12, VA
Benjamin F., laborer, 19, VA
Joseph T., 6, VA
John, 2, VA
JOHNSON
Eliza, 28, VA

350 – KEFFER
John, carpenter, 38, PA
Victoria, 20, VA

351 – O'NEIL
John, laborer, 35, Ire.
Mary, 35, Ire.
Ann, 2, VA
LAHOE
Michael, 14, Ire.
John, 12, Ire.
O'NEIL
Martin, 10, Ire.

352 – BENEDICT
Samuel, farmer-merchant, 62, CN
Ellen M., 58, NY
George K., clerk, 34, NY
Park, clerk, 19, NY
CUNNINGHAM
John S., civil engineer, 32, NJ
Helen M., 26, NY
Eveline, 1, VA

353 — ALLEN
William H., lockkeeper, 43, VA
Sarah, 43, VA
Mary B., 21, VA
William H., laborer, 19, VA
Frances (female), 16, VA
John J., 15, VA
George M., 10, VA
Willie E. (female), 7, VA
Andrew, 2, VA

354 — TINSLEY
Madison, farmer, 56, VA
Sarah, 48, VA
Isaac, boatman, 23, VA
Joshua, boatman, 20, VA
Augustus, laborer, 24, VA
William H., laborer, 18, VA
Robert H., 15, VA
Caroline, 14, VA
Eliza, 10, VA
Minerva J., 8, VA
James M., 5, VA
George B., 2, VA

355 — SMOOT
William A., carpenter, 39, NC
Margaret H., 41, VA
John W., 10, VA
Georgeanna (female), 7, VA
Sophia C., 4, VA
Mary F., 2, VA
Thomas W., 8 mo., VA

356 — THOMPSON
George P., farm manager, 27, VA
THORNTON
Aylett H., M.D., 42, VA
Martha (HUDSON?), 28, VA

357 — WHITTINGTON
John, farm manager, 35, VA
Nancy M. (SHOEMAKER), 24, VA
James L., 5, VA
John B., 4, VA
Charles, 5 mo., VA
CLEMENS
Elizabeth, 22, VA
W. Catherine, 1, VA

358 — TEAYS
James S., farmer, 43, VA
Mary A., 40, VA
Stephen T., laborer, 20, VA
John H., 19, VA
Mary C., 13, VA
James W., 10, VA
Alice E., 8, VA
Martha H., 6, VA
Parthenia J., 3, VA
THOMAS
Elizabeth R., 33, VA
James S. TAYES married Mary Ann THOMAS,
26 Nov. 1838 by E. Hewes Field, Min.

359 — LOGANS
Solomon (mulatto), waiter, 50, VA
Catherine (mulatto), 34, VA

HANES
Sophia (mulatto), 10, VA
Catherine (mulatto), 8, VA

360 — CAPEHART
Charles C., hotel landlord, 39, VA
Mary E., 31, VA

361 — DOUGLAS
Jacob, laborer, 35, VA
America, 25, VA

362 — WILKERSON
Lewis, carpenter, 27, VA
Mary B., 24, VA
Martha, 21, VA
Lawrence A., apprentice, 18, VA
Sarah, 51, VA

363 — ALLEN
James M., cooper, 35, VA
Mary, 36, VA
Charles, 10, VA
Polly, 9, VA
Elizabeth, 8, VA
Josephine, 6, VA
Samuel, 5, VA
Henry, 4, VA
Mildred, 3, VA
Lilburn (male), 1, VA

364 — SEASHOAL
Jeremiah, wheelwright, 35, PA
Mary E., 32, PA
Samuel W., 11, PA
Barbara A., 7, VA
Mary E., 6, VA
James A., 1, VA
SMITH
Michael, carriage maker, 25, PA
BLACK
William, blacksmith, 33, PA
JONES
George M., 26, KY
BERRY
R.D., blacksmith, 25, NY
COPLEN
John R., wheelwright, 24

365 — PARSONS
Columbus, laborer, 26, VA
Martha (PERSINGER), 30, VA
Mary F., 12, VA
Albert, 9, VA
Uriah (male), 8, VA
William H., 6, VA
Virginia F., 5, VA
Lillia (female), 2, VA

366 — JOHNSON,
Jesse F., saddler, 38, NC
Susan J. (BARRETT),34, VA
Charles, 9, VA
William, 6, VA
Ellen J., 3, VA
PERSINGER
Almeda, 14, VA
VANDINE
Isiah, 25, VA

367 — OVERSHINER
John, wagonmaker, 47, VA
Margaret, 42, VA
George M., wagonmaker, 21, VA
James M., wagonmaker, 19, VA
Frances E., 12, VA
Timothy T., 7, VA
Margaret, 4, VA
COLLINS
Andrew, carpenter, 24, VA

368 — MILLER
William J., shoemaker, 31, VA
Ruth A., 26, VA
George, 15, VA
Minerva, 13, VA
William J., 10, VA
Daniel, 8, VA
Charles, 6, VA
Sarah, 4, VA
John W., 1, VA
McGHEE
John H., 26, Eng.

369 — CASTER
William, laborer, 35, Ger.
Amazetta, 20, VA
Mary C., 2, VA

370 — CANTERBERRY
John, carpenter, 43, VA
Catharine, 42, VA
Mary, 18, VA
Margaret, 15, VA
DEATON
Charles, laborer, 26, VA

371 — SHEASHOAL
Isaac, carriage maker, 30, PA.:; America, 26, VA
Fanny W., 6, VA
John A., 4, VA

372 — HENSON
William H., blacksmith, 28, VA
Mary, 28, VA
Mary V., 8, VA
Fanny, 2, VA
Eliza B., 4 mo., VA
NICHOLS
Samuel S., gunsmith, 49, VA

373 — McCLARY
Samuel, stonemason, 50, Ire.
Elizabeth, 50, Ire.
TOMMY
Bridget, 14, Ire.

374 — ROCK
Anderson, merchant, 34, VA
Eliza, 30, VA
George, 7, VA
Daniel, 5, VA
Sagernia (female), 1, VA

375 — LASLEY
  Ivy (male), gent, 65, VA
  Willie (female), 40, VA
  Sarah, 24, VA
  Louisa, 22, VA
  Willard (female), 20, VA
  Willie (female), 13, VA

376 — HUMPHREYS
  John E., cooper, 35, VA
  Sally, 30, VA
  Betsy J., 15, VA
  Victoria, 12, VA
  Fountain A. (male), 7, VA
  Martha, 3, VA

377 — CARPENTER
  Peter, laborer, 30, VA
  Mary, 27, VA
  William J., 8, VA
  Elias, 6, VA
  John E., 4, VA
  Anderson C., 1, VA
  DAILEY
  Clarissa, cook, 30, VA

378 — HOLCOLM
  James, laborer, 18, VA
  CASH
  Benjamin, laborer, 21, VA
  Powhatan, laborer, 40, VA
  MITHER
  Andrew, laborer, 28, VA

378A — CA[P]EHEART
  Daniel, shoemaker, 26, PA
  Rebecca, 25, VA
  Eliza, 6, VA
  William, 4, VA
  Fanny, 2, VA
  Daniel, 6 mo., VA

379 — HUDSON
  Alonzo I.M., Episcopal minister, 43, VT
  Mary, 34, OH
  Samuel M., 11, OH
  John, 5, OH
  Mary, 3, OH
  Lilly, 3 mo., VA
  FINDLEY
  Kate, 16, Pa or IA

380 — SCOTT
  Andrew, carpenter, 40, OH
  Mary A., 36, VA
  Oliver, laborer, 21, VA
  Susan, 12, VA
  Mary, 3, VA
  McWIGGING
  John, boatman, 32, VA

381 — WEBB
  William H., lumberman, 38, NY
  Hannah, 32, OH
  William F., 11, OH
  Theodore F., 9, OH
  Hazen L. (male), 5, VA
  Emma, 3, VA

Charles, 1, VA
WEBB
  Jeremiah, sawyer, 75, NY

382 — VAUGHN (or Straughn?)
  William W., boatman, 37, VA
  Catherine, 34, KY
  YOUNG
  Ovia (female), 10, OH
  STRAUGHN
  Molly, 84, VA

383 — TURNER
  John P., farmer, 64, MA
  Helena M. (THOMPSON), 55, VA
  Sarah F., 28, VA
  Charles, toll collector, 26, VA
  Martha, 24, VA
  John, student, 20, VA
  James Mc, 17, VA

384 — VICARS
  Watson, farmer, 52, KY
  Eliza, 38, VA
  James, boatman, 21, VA
  Mary A., 16, VA
  John, 15, VA
  Laura, 13, VA
  Willie (female), 7, VA

385 — PORTER
  Benjamin F, schoolteacher, 36, VA
  Mary, 30, VA
  James S., 9, VA
  Guy P., 8, VA
  Blanche F., 6, VA
  Helen J., 5, VA
  John F., 4, VA
  Fredrick, 3, VA
  G. Andrew, 2, VA
  Unnamed male, 1 mo., VA

386 — WILSON
  William S., shipmaster, 41, VA
  Sarah, 39, VA
  Lillian, 11, VA
  See (?) (female), 9, VA
  William H., 6, VA
  Hazen H. (male), 4, VA
  Edwin, 2, VA
  PROFIT
  Martha, 50, Russ.
  STRAWES
  Grandison, laborer, 28, Russ.
  GILLERLAND
  Samuel, laborer, 42, VA

387 — HANSFORD
  John, gent, 62, VA
  Charles B., 26, VA
  Carol C. (female), clerk, 24, VA
  Victoria F.C., 22, VA
  Centhia N., 19, VA
  MOSS
  Charles D., M.D., 30, VA

381 — CAPEHART
  Stephen, farmer, 28, VA

Susan, 26, VA
Willie (male), 3, VA

390 — WILSON
  Samuel, farmer, 58, VA
  Parthenia, 56, VA
  Parthenia J., 22, VA
  Martha A., 21, VA
  Oliver, student, 17, VA
  Sarah A., 12, VA
  CHILTON
  [George S., clerk, 27, VA
  [Hannah E., 27, VA
      [m. 1860]

391 — CREASEY
  Wyatt, farm manager, 35, VA
  Susan, 33, VA
  Susan V., 8, VA
  Ella C., 5, VA
  William E., 2, VA
  WELCH
  Susan, 72, VA

392 — FORD
  William, farmer, 61, Eng.
  Jane, 62, Eng.
  Mary C., 13, Eng.
  FOSTER
  Charles, clerk, 26, NY
  Mary J., 25, PA
  Alice, 1 mo., VA

393 — BROWN
  James M., laborer, 52, Eng.
  Mary, 52, Eng.
  John, laborer, 18, NY
  Sarah A., 15, NY
  Hester, 11, PA
  YOUNG
  John, laborer, 38, Eng.
  McCOEN
  James, laborer, 50, Ire.

394 — THOMPSON
  Benjamin S., gent, 40, VA
  Elizabeth, 36, VA
  Acameria (male), merchant, 18, VA
  Linn (female), 15, VA
  Fanny L. 10, VA
  William, 5, VA

395 — MILLER
  Wilson, laborer, 27, VA
  Elizabeth, 36, VA
  Mary E.H., 4, VA
  William, 3, VA
  Anna, 1, VA

396 — BEARD
  Thomas J., farmer, 41, VA
  Sarah A.E. (OGBURN), 38, VA
  Clayton C., 13, VA
  Nancy M., 11, VA
  Adam, 9, VA

397 – CARTER
Patrick, laborer, 30, Ire.
Mary, 28, VA
John C., 4, VA
William H., 2, VA
Mary A., 1, VA

398 – TOMPKINS
Beverly, farmer, 26, VA
Sally (Sarah H. THOMPSON?), 20, VA
Helena, 2, VA
Willie (female), 11 mo., VA

399 – CREASY
Charlotte, 50, Ger.
Theodore, laborer, 19, Ger.
BAZING
John, 19, Ger.

400 – LOVELL
John, shoemaker, 24, VA
Farlenia (female), 20, NC
William J., 4, NC
John H., 3, VA
Mary J., 1 mo., VA

401 – WOOD
[Quincy, laborer, 25, NC
[Martha (HIGH), 20, NC
[m. 1860]
Wiley H. (male), 2, NC

402 – THOMPSON
Elizabeth H., 35, KY
Willie, 9, Cal.
HUIE
James B., farmer, 61, VA

403 – RUST
Samuel, farmer, 52, VA
Elizabeth (RUST), 41, VA
James W., student, 16, VA
Alfred H., 13, VA
Bushrod S. (male), 11, VA
Rebecca, 8, VA
John F., 5, VA
Richard L., 3, VA

404 – GREGORY
Henry, grocer, 21, VA
Sarah E., 18, VA

405 – RUST
Richard, farmer, 36, VA
Feletia M. (female), 27, VA
Emma A., 5, VA
James S., 3, VA
Mary E., 6 mo., VA

406 – DUDDING
Joseph, farmer, 59, VA
Catherine, 46, VA; John, laborer, 26, VA
Margaret, 24, VA
Lethe, 20, VA
William S., 17, VA
Mary, 13, VA
Nancy, 11, VA
Feletia (female), 7, VA

BYRD
Moses, schoolteacher, 26, VA

407 – SHELTON
Thomas M., farmer, 45, VA
Ann, 39, KY

408 – MARKHAM
Benjamin D., farm manager, 27, VA
Eliza A., 27, VA
Dolly A., 7, VA

409 – DUDDING
Nancy, farmer, 48, VA
Leander, laborer, 31, VA
Joseph, laborer, 30, VA
Alonzo, 13, VA
CONEY
[George, laborer, 26, VA
[Elizabeth, 22, VA
[m. 1860]

410 – DUDDING
Benjamin F., farmer, 25, VA
Martha M., 22, VA
Nancy J., 3, VA

411 – LILLY
Napolean B., farmer, 41, VA
Catherine, 33, VA
Elizabeth J., 11, VA
William N., 5, VA

412 – RIDDLE
George, carpenter, 42, VA
Louisa, 30, VA
Mary J., 8, VA
Nancy A., 5, VA
Rachael E., 3, VA
Martha E., 1, VA

413 – PEDAGRIER (?)
Margaret, 42
Isabella, 12
Elizabeth, 11
Catherine, 9
Emiline, 2

414 – THOMAS
James M., farmer, 27, VA
Mary J., 20, VA

415 – LEWIS
Thomas A., farmer, 51, VA
Mary (STOCKTON), 41, VA
William S., student M.D., 21, VA
DOTSON
Napolean, laborer, 16, VA

416 – BROOKS
Lawson S., farmer, 67, VA
Catherine, 71, VA
Napolean B., laborer, 23, VA
Robert B., laborer, 30, VA

417 – SHAWVER
George M., laborer, 46, VA
Sophia, 35, VA

Mary J., 16, VA
Marshall F., 14, VA
James M., 10, VA
Sarah E., 8, VA
Samuel A., 2, VA

418 – SHAWVER
James, laborer, 35, VA
Miriam, 34, VA
John L., laborer, 16, VA
Gradison, 15, VA
William, 12, VA
James A., 10, VA
Joseph H., 9, VA
Martha A., 4, VA
Levi, 8 mo., VA
SHAWVER
Sarah, 94, VA
Jane, 70, VA

419 – SHAWVER
John, laborer, 30, VA
Martha J. (blind), 24, VA

420 – MORRIS
Reuben, farmer, 40, VA
Pomelia, 41, VA
George H., laborer, 20, VA
William S., laborer, 18, VA
John, laborer, 17, VA
Mary F., 9, VA

421 – GRANT
Roswell, farmer, 60, KY
Elizabeth, 24, KY
Susan, 19, KY
Thomas, laborer, 18, KY

422 – WILLIAMS
Lewis, farmer, 36, VA
Melinda, 35, VA
Elizabeth, 14, VA
John C., 5, VA
Judith F., 4, VA
James, 6 mo., VA

423 – WHITTINGTON
Stark, farmer, 54, VA
Rhoda, 38, VA
James B., laborer, 18, VA
Agnes, 8, VA
Virginia, 7, VA
William A., 4, VA
John, 1, VA

424 – WRIGHT
Elizabeth, 48, VA
Hamilton, boatman, 28, VA
James, 15, VA
Derensia (female), 14, VA

425 – FOWLER
[James, laborer, 26, VA
[Magdeline, 25, VA
[m. 1860]

426 — HARRISON
James M. (H.?), farmer, 33, VA
Jula E. (McCOWN), 40, VA
Cordelia S., 11, VA
James W., 8, VA
William S., 7, VA
Alvin F., 5, VA
Barbara S.A., 3, VA
Verbinia C. (female), 1, VA

427 — DUDDING
Sampson, farmer, 37, VA
Eliza A., 24, VA
Mary S., 1 mo., VA

428 — CABELL
Samuel I., farmer, 53, VA

429 — SHOEMAKER
James, farmer, 65, VA
Asenia (female), 55, VA
Richmond W. (male), laborer, 37, VA
Susan, 34, VA
Charles W., laborer, 19, VA
Catherine, 17, VA

430 — WEBB
[Thomas B., farmer, 24, VA
[Frances E. (CROUCH), 19, VA
    [m. 1859]

431 — FINNEY
William, farm manager, 38, VA
Elizabeth (PRESTON), 32, VA
Lethe (female), 12, VA
Mary, 9, VA
Josaphine, 7, VA
Charles, 5, VA
William, 2, VA
Victoria, 5 mo., VA

SELECTED BIBLIOGRAPHY

Atkinson, George W. *History of Kanawha Co.* Charleston, W. Va.,, W. Va. Journal-1876

Boatner, Mark M. III. *Civil War Dictionary* .New York, N. Y., David McKay Co. 1959

Cartmell, T.K. *Shenandoah Pioneers and Their Descendants.* Virginia Book Co.

Civil War Times Magazine. Selected Articles 1970-1988

Cohen, Stan. *Historic Springs of the Virginias.* Charleston, W. Va., Pictorial Hist. Pub. Co. 1987

Cohen, Stan. *Kanawha County Images.* Charleston, W. Va. Pictorial Histories Pub. Co. 1988

Comstock, Jim, Comp. *Hardesty's W. Va. Counties Kanawha and Putnam.* Richwood, W. Va., W. Va. Hillbilly 1973

Cox, Jacob D. *Military Reminiscences of the Civil War — vol. I* New York: Charles Scribner's Sons 1900

Dabney, B. L. *Life and Campaigns of General T. J. (Stonewall) Jackson.* Harrisburg: Sprinkle Publications 1977

Dayton, Ruth Woods. *Pioneers and Their Homes on the Upper Kanawha.* Charleston, W. Va.: W. Va. Pub. Co. 1947

DeGruyter, Julius. *The Kanawha Spectator — Vol. I.* Charleston, W. Va. Jarrett Printing Co. 1953

Dickinson, Jack L. *8th Virginia Cavalry.* Lynchburg, Va.: H. E. Howard, Inc. 1986

Hale, John P. *History of the Great Kanawha Valley — 2 Vols.* Madison, Wis.: Brant, Fuller & Co. 1891

Laidley, William S. *History of Charleston & Kanawha Co.* Chicago: Richmond-Arnold Pub. Co. 1911

Lowry, Terry D. *Battle of Scary Creek* Charleston, W. Va.: Pictorial Histories Pub. Co. 1982

Lowry, Terry D. *22nd Virginia Inf.* Lynchburg, Va.: H.E. Howard Inc. 1988

MacCorkle, William A. *The White Sulphur Springs.* Neale Publishing Co. 1916

Martin, David G. *Jackson's Valley Campaign 1861-1862.* New York: W. H. Smith Pub. Inc. 1988

Methodism and Early Days in Stephen City, Va. 1732-1905.

Winchester, Va.: Geo. F. Norton Pub. Co. 1906

Quarles, Garland R., Ed. *What I Know About Winchester Recollections of W. G. Russell 1800-1891.* Staunton, Va.: McGuire Pub. Co. 1972

Rice, Otis K. *Charleston and the Kanawha Valley.* Woodland Hills, Cal.: Windsor Pub. Inc. 1981

Schlidt, John W. *Hunter Holmes McGuire Doctor in Gray.* Chewsville, Md.: 1986.

Scott, J. L. *36th Virginia Inf.* Lynchburg, Va.: H. E. Howard, Inc. 1987

St. Albans Historical Society Journal. Selected Articles, 1972-1988

Stutler, Boyd B. *W. Va. in the Civil War.* Charleston: Educations Foundation 1955

Upper Vandalia Hist. Society Journal. Selected Articles, 1962-1988

Wallace, George S. *Cabell County Annals and Families* Richmond: Garrett and Massie Pub. 1935

Wallace, Lee A., Jr. *A Guide to Va. Mil. Organizations 1861-1865.* H. E. Howard, Inc. Rev. 1935

Wayland, John W. *Twenty Five Chapters on the Shenandoah Valley.* Harrisonburg, Va.: C. J. Carrier Co. 1976

West Virginia Historical and Antiquarian Society Journal. January 1897

West Virginia Historical Magazine 1901-1905. Selected Articles

Wilson, James G. and Fisk, John, Eds., 6 Vols. Appleton's Cyclopedia of Amer. Biog.; New York: D. Appleton and Co. 1888

Winchester-Frederick County Civil War Centennial Commission. *Civil War Battles in Winchester and Frederick County, Va.* 1960

Wintz, William D. *Nitro The WWI Boom Town.* South Charleston, W.Va. Jallamap Pub. Co. 1985.

Wintz, William D. Ed. *Recollections and Reflections of Mollie Hansford — 1828-1900.* Charleston: Quick Copy Dupl. 1976.

INDEX